CODEPENDENCY:

PowerLoss
SoulLoss

CODEPENDENCY:

PowerLoss
SoulLoss

Dorothy May, Ph.D.

Whales' Tales Press
Paulist Press

Published by
Whales' Tales Press
160 Wildwood • Lake Forest, IL 60045
1-800-428-9507

Paulist Press
997 Macarthur Blvd. • Mahwah, NJ 07438
201/825-7300

Please note that *Codependency: PowerLoss SoulLoss* is not a substitute for individual psychotherapy.

Printed in the United States of America

Library of Congress Catalog Number: 94-60569

ISBN 1-882195-02-7 (Whales' Tales Press)
ISBN 0-8091-3532-9 (Paulist Press)

Cover Illustration by Chris Reeves
Text Design by Chris Harnesk

I dedicate this book to
My mother — her mother — her mother...
My father — his father — his father...
My siblings, Tony, Hob, June...
and unto the generations...

To my husband Don...
and to our children,
Michael, Cyndi and Steven...
and unto the generations...

This book
belongs
to

_____

CONTENTS

ACKNOWLEDGMENTS

I have lived out this book for a very long time. Through it I have found and expressed my own soul's voice. On my journey, there have been other voices who have encouraged and supported my efforts. With heartfelt gratitude, my appreciation goes to:

Dr. Kathleen Whalen FitzGerald, whose skillful guidance and loving, consistent support afforded me the confidence I needed to make concrete my professional and personal experience. Had it not been for her, this book would have been stillborn.

Dick Sparks and Don Brophy at Paulist Press, whose compassionate, patient understanding has kept me on my creative path. I am ever grateful.

My personal friends, clients and students who've offered me their experience and their hearts.

My readers and reviewers, Gail D., Janet M., Jim H., Julie B., Kathy S., Mary Ann C., Terry M., Sara H., and an anonymous reader, all of whom made this book feel real to me and loved me through my discouragement with the revision process.

Chris Harnesk, my designer, whose steady and loving energy kept me grounded.

Chris Leiper-Reeves, whose artistic talent and loving hand graces our cover.

Sister Kathleen O'Connell, my editor, whose competency and kindness allowed me to run the final pages in relative peace.

INTRODUCTION

Codependency is an idea whose time has come, a condition of our times. Codependency has become popularized and generalized to the point where it is an almost meaningless term.

When a concept has captured, capsulized and crystallized the experience of so many Americans, however, it must be examined and made part of our literary heritage as well as recorded as an integral part of the American experience. This book attempts to do this.

Psychology and psychological terms have become more and more widely accepted, but codependency is more than a psychological term and process. Concepts of codependency have touched a deep need for transcendence and a need for deeper, clearer and more defined relationships and boundaries — with God, with each other and with ourselves.

To define codependency, we must see that it is multifaceted and far-reaching. The issues of separation and attachment are central to any definition of codependency. The ways in which we teach our children to separate from the group, beginning with the family, that is, to individuate, has to do with allowing them to think for themselves and to make effective decisions in a world that begs for innovative, competent leaders. The ways in which we teach them to attach to others has to do with helping them to feel safe and secure within themselves in the midst of a world where citizens feel unsafe and insecure. Children who grow up feeling physically, emotionally or spiritually unsafe, unprotected and undernourished, cannot return to a society the nourishment they have not received. Only when people feel connected to, a part of and vital to their society, can they participate fully in the workings of that society.

Codependency is a large-scale societal failure to teach children the self-development and the personal empowerment it takes to direct their lives in a meaningful manner. People who develop inner power have the ability to initiate change and to influence their own lives as well as the lives of others.

In taking their own power from our children, we rob them of a vital life force. We rob them and, consequently, the world of their soul.

If we lose our soul, we lose our power and we become as walking dead. Power is a moving, animating force within us which creates our aliveness. Power provides the energy that moves our soul in the world. Soul-power becomes personal power when it creates energy for aliveness. The ways in which power is misused and abused in families and individuals result in disempowerment. In this book, we have translated these ideas into practical aspects of the codependent quandary.

Codependency affects people in all aspects of their lives: work, relationships, marriage, children. Codependency is the end result of an acquisitive society where more is better, faster is the norm and nothing is ever enough.

Codependency shows itself in extremes, which we call addiction. We have used our addictions to pretend we have no choices and thus no responsibility for our own lives. We have used our addictions to distance ourselves socially and emotionally from one another as well as from ourselves — and ultimately, from our God. Codependency is the root addiction of all — a disempowerment that creates a final alienation from all that gives life meaning.

Education is the first step in the journey to self-knowledge, self-direction and personal empowerment. When we no longer are alienated, our souls will return. This book attempts to answer some of the many questions that arise in the minds of people who are searching for their own souls, seeking out their own truth and willing to learn new ways.

All of the questions presented here are real questions posed by real people, like you. The basic material is drawn from two sources. One is a two-year series of workshops on codependency issues, sponsored by the Institute for Recovery in Deerfield, Illinois. Nearly two thousand people have participated in these workshops.

A second source of material is based on my own practice over the past eight years. As a practicing psychologist, I have seen perhaps a thousand people who exhibit codependent behavior or who live a codependent life style. They come from all walks of life and cross all strata of society. Some are from alcoholic homes. Others are not. But all are codependents in pain and all are lost children in need of relief. All want to cope with life in less stressful, freer and healthier ways.

It is my hope that you, the reader, will join me and countless others on the road to discovering freedom, hope and power.

"The real voyage of discovery lies not in seeking new landscapes but in having new eyes."

— Marcel Proust

*A note on style. Throughout this book, codependents will be referred to as "she" or "he" at random. Codependency knows no gender.

BEFORE YOU BEGIN...

A Personal Message from Dorothy

Have you ever noticed that when you get a new book, your stomach begins to rev-up and your throat gets tight? You begin to build up to a pitch as you ravenously devour the contents of your latest treasure.

In the pit of your mind, you just know that here you will find the answer. I'd spent a lifetime looking for the answer before I realized that there is no one answer. But there are some answers. I offer you some answers to whet your appetite. These are only my answers. You have your own truth. I hope this book will be your own personal journey to your truth.

This book is yours. You can do with it what you like. I invite you to make it your own. Write your name in it — draw all around your name, to celebrate it. One way to make it fully yours is to create a personal journal. If there is a single therapeutic tool that has consistently worked, it is journaling.

There are many good guides on journaling, but here is one way to begin. Get a beautiful notebook, a book of blank pages that feels good to you, the right color, the right size, paper that you love. Use this text as a jumping-off place and write in it your thoughts, reflections, feelings, drawings, scribblings and whatever comes up for you. Carry it with you wherever you go. Writing the truth is very healing. Take this book and your journals to your therapy sessions; spend time alone in your private room with them; take them down to the lake when you seek peace; and meditate on them in your quiet times.

I encourage you to explore the ideas presented. I ask you to experiment with different media...talk, draw, paint, color, use photographs, sculpt with clay, listen to music, stretch your body, dance your way around this material. Throughout this work, I ask you to extend your range of experience, to open yourselves to new ideas, to respond strongly, to form your own opinions, to test the water, to feel your feet on a new path. Let your creative, spontaneous, natural child out to play. Accept the honest reality that comes forth.

Speaking of play, I've noticed that none of the many questions people have asked includes the idea of play. Although there are some codependents who truly know how to play, most of us simply don't think of this as an adult activity. We ordinarily think of play as child's work, an activity done for its own sake, without a particular purpose. It just feels good. I'd like you to think about play also as a form of exploration and experimentation. Play as an attitude, an orientation. Play as an opening of the mind and heart.

Writings on codependency place much emphasis on pain, wounding and trouble. We seem to leave little room for positive feelings of joy, pleasure, freedom, delight, enthusiasm, excitement. I invite you to experience the full extent of your thoughts, feelings and actions. The full range of your life. The fullness of your own, original soul.

After each question, there will be a space for you to make your own personal applications of the material. I've included some questions for you, but you're not locked into using them. Some questions will not include any comments from me at all. Feel free to use, change or discard at will my comments.

There may be some questions which seem to have no meaning to you at this time. Their relevance may come up for you later. It's a good idea to put a book aside — any book— for three to six months or even a year. When you pick it up again, things will jump out at you that you hadn't noticed earlier.

There may be some "hot spots" for you here. Notice the point in the book at which you can't read any more and need to put it down. These hot spots are important to your growth. Keep a record of them as you make this book your own. Have fun with it. Digest it.

Pay no attention to the voices in your head that say, "What do you know? You're no expert." You are the only expert who counts. If you hear, "Don't write in books," don't listen. Truth is, writers love interaction with readers.

There is no hurry. You have all the time you need. Sometimes you may need to reread a section. Put a paper clip on the top of the page or a slip of paper at the place you want. You have my permission to disagree and to form your own opinions. Forget all the old rules you learned about not making mistakes. Learning includes the willingness to be wrong. Make up your own rules as you go along. After all, someone had to make up the original rules. Who's to say we can't change them? From time to time, I'll be speaking to you in a narrative way. You'll recognize my voice by my signature D, as it is on the bottom of this paragraph. I'd like to hear your voice, too, so write to me personally with your questions, responses, comments; in any form you like. I'll respond to your communications. Information on where to reach me is on page 291.

PART ONE

Loss of Soul: Disempowerment

Roots in the Family

Core Issues

Denial

Who it Affects

How it Affects Us

Characteristics of Codependency

LOSS OF SOUL: DISEMPOWERMENT

I invite you to come with me on a journey to empowerment and freedom. Close your inner eyes and imagine that you and I are sitting together with a small group of other voyagers. My eyes travel around our circle and I welcome you to the pages of our classroom. Together we will explore the dark, unknown continent of codependency.

You are hesitant but curious. You feel intuitively that what you are about to begin will lead to greater *freedom*.

That is your hope...but it is not a certainty. Your eagerness is tinged with anxiety. Eagerness and anxiety will walk side by side on your journey to where your soul awaits. It is a place deep within your knowing self. It is the home of your power... that lives in your soul and animates your life.

For a moment, right now, take a few deep breaths. Hold a pencil loosely in your dominant hand. Close your eyes and think of the word:

POWER

After a few moments, open your eyes and write as many words, phrases and sentences as come to you when you think of the word: Power.

A few of mine:

power over	ability	greatness
influence	capacity	authority
dominate	aggression	control
command	potent	energy
enable	dynamic	

When you have finished, look at the kinds of associations you make about power. What does this say about you?

Personal empowerment is the result of being internally power-*full*. Being full of power means, not to have "power-over" another, but being full of *energy*.

Having the authority of one's own power creates an ability or capacity to act effectively and to impact our world. Ralph Waldo

Emerson wrote, "The power which resides in the individual is not new in nature and none but he knows what that is which he can do, nor does he know until he has tried."

Codependency seems to be transmitted through the air like a virus, or passed around by a kind of psychological osmosis. Perhaps we can pass our empowerment around, too. If enough people gain back their own power, then society will change for the better. "As it is with the individual, so it is with the nation." (Roosevelt)

Codependency is a condition in which the loss of power produces a subsequent alienation from self, from others and, ultimately, from God. We become disconnected from our own experience and our own inner knowing. We feel trapped, stuck, chained to our helplessness. We are victims.

The disconnection I'm talking about occurs first in our childhood, within the crucible of the family. Let us insert a word of caution here. *The family of origin material presented here is not meant to blame, only to understand.* The family is the context out of which we come. The actual people who *happen* to be your parents, siblings and other relatives were acting only on what they themselves had learned.

When we talk about parents, siblings and other relatives, we are speaking of the symbolic meaning of those people to the developing child. Resources within a family are things like love, attention, money, food, time, space and energy. The adults in a family system hold the power to distribute such resources to the children. Those with the resources are those with the power, the power to give or to withhold what the child needs. The ways in which power is portioned-out in the family determine to a large extent the health of that family. In some families, resources are carefully dispensed and in effect, rationed according to some larger plan of which no one is quite aware. The ways in which power is used, misused and abused results in empowerment or disempowerment. We all come from different families, yet there are common threads among our families. The commonalities are woven into the fabric called codependency. D

ROOTS IN THE FAMILY

Question One

I don't know what it's like to feel power inside of me. I do know helplessness. I do know smallness and worthlessness. I need to understand why I feel so ashamed of myself. It comes up in everything I do.

You may have come from a toxic home and your power was taken away from you a piece at a time. As your power was taken away, your soul left, too, a piece at a time. In a toxic home, there is misuse and abuse of power. It begins with one dominant person who is *always* right and one submissive person who is *always* wrong, with few adults around whom a child can imitate.

People in this type of family use ridicule as a means of social control. Family members laugh at others, especially those who are different or those who are in trouble.

The child at first thinks his family has a good sense of humor. Other people seem wrong and his family seems right. But soon he realizes that his family also makes fun of him when he is feeling hurt. He begins to keep his head down when he is walking and doesn't often look people in the eye. He keeps on smiling, no matter how he feels. He is learning shame. He is losing soul.

The *We-Them* mentality speaks loud and clear: to belong to our family, you must do what we say is *right*. We know what is right and those outside the family are *all wrong*.

The world view is that people take sides to win or to lose. Winners crow, triumphant; losers cry, ashamed. The world outside the family is dangerous and deceptive. We have to stay within the protection of the family. Parents say things like, "No one will ever stick by you the way we do, and be on our side, or else..."

This form of social control effectively ties and gags members of the family, keeps the status quo and allows no changes. Good for those on top! This type of family is often run by one Great Dictator, the one who sets the rigid rules. The rules are reinforced by the Chief Enabler, usually the spouse. Children learn early that *no one crosses the King!* This is a shame-based family system.

Think about…

Who was King in your family?

Who made that person King?

What were two messages from your family that expressed the We-Them mentality?

Question Two

What do you mean by shame-based?

A child becomes familiar with the feeling of shame, even though he cannot at first name or label it. He may have feelings of worthlessness, of a hollowness in the pit of the stomach, and of being small. He may feel like a snail or a slug, or like he is shrinking down and looking up at another person. He may have a terror of exposure, a feeling of naked vulnerability — like walking down a street without clothes.

That feeling, created in childhood, lies deep inside of us. It is the feeling we are most terrified of and will go to any lengths to protect and to avoid.

Unconsciously, when shame-based people have experiences as adults that are positive and self-validating, they do not recognize those experiences as positive. There are no associations or "hooks" to which they can attach those good feelings. So they keep searching.

They also do things they know are wrong, such as stealing from Mom's purse in childhood, using drugs later on, lying so that they don't reveal themselves. This is how they bring shame on themselves.

No one would do this consciously. The feeling of shame is so deep, familiar and constant that it becomes like an addiction. Shame brings a sick flop in the stomach, a black lump in the chest and a tight wire around the throat. Shame-based people crave and search out that feeling and do not recognize the good feelings of self-worth that come along. So they crawl on, unaware that they are crawling or craving. And the soul begins to close its eyes.

Think about...

How do you keep yourself in shame?

When did your soul first begin to close its eyes?

What happened?

How old were you?

Question Three

What is addiction to shame?

Addiction to shame occurs in ways. Overspending can end in shame when we are surrounded by beautiful things which give no pleasure. When the bills come due and become a mountain of debt, we feel shame. Though we felt a great high when we filled our shopping carts, our inability to control our spending activates our shame. This process can be seen most clearly in drinking behavior. It's a cycle. We begin with fear. We see that fear leads to pleasing others. Pleasing others leads to anger. Anger leads to rebellion and belligerence. When we are belligerent, we feel guilty. Then we either put others up or put ourselves down. There has to be a winner and a loser.

When we do this, our basic, core-shame is activated. We are so familiar with the feelings associated with shame that these feelings lock into place easily. But shame spirals downward until it is so painful — then the addiction takes over. If the addiction is to alcohol, we feel so much fear and shame that we drink...we become ashamed of our drinking...and the cycle begins again.

Think about…

Recall an incident in which your fear led to pleasing others.

Did you complete the cycle that time?

What happened?

Did you experience anger?

Did you recognize the anger?

Did you express the anger?

How?

Question Four

I don't understand shame. Is this guilt? How does it work?

Shame seems to be layered under guilt. Shame is connected with *feeling worthless* while guilt is connected with *behavior*. Shame and guilt are connected through fear.

Shame and fear are bedrock, biological human emotions. Guilt is an overlay of societal injunctions (rules and laws). Shame and fear are not taught. They come up when we feel threatened, emotionally or physically. Guilt, on the other hand, arises as a result of breaking the rules we've been *taught* are *right*. It works like this:

A person begins in fear with shame underneath. To hide his fear, he begins people-pleasing behavior. When this doesn't take away his fear, he becomes angry. "I can't please you anyway — no matter what I do, it's not good enough." His anger leads to defiance, belligerence and rebellion. This in turn, leads to guilt. "I *should not* feel so angry. It's not *right*." Being angry breaks a rule.

His inner conflict finally leads him to tell himself, righteously, "Why *should* I feel guilty?" This angry statements is followed by fear: "No matter what I do, I'm going to be in trouble." Then, "I must be a creep to feel this way. No one else feels this bad..." "Why did I do that? For heaven's sake, I gotta get over it!" These are self-shaming statements. These feelings and thoughts lead to his basic core of shame. He may try other behaviors to cover the shame but once the core-shame is activated, it spirals ever downward.

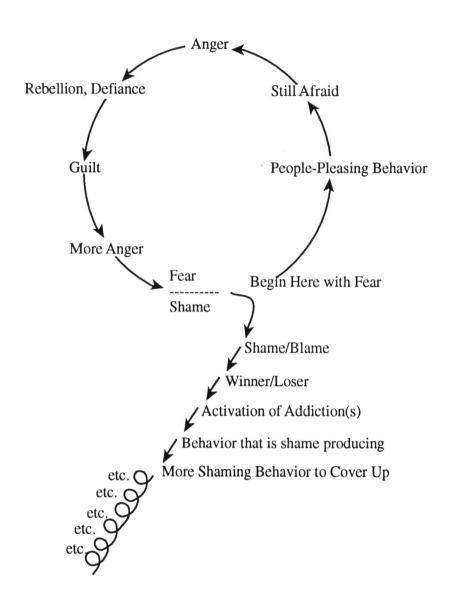

Question Five

My family was different. We didn't use ridicule or rigid rules. But there were people yelling all the time. And I don't seem to be able to carry on a normal life without fear haunting me at every step. Is it me?

No, it isn't you. You may have come from an anger-based family, which uses another form of disempowerment. In these families, people are either mad or afraid. Scratch an angry person and you'll touch fear. In these types of family systems, feelings are not spoken. They are pushed deep down inside. People are not aware of their feelings.

When we are unaware of our feelings, we act them out to relieve the tension and pain. When people feel afraid, they act angry. Jill sets unrealistic and unnecessarily harsh rules about early curfew for her well-behaved seventeen-year-old. If the adolescent comes home even ten minutes late, Jill yells and screams and grounds the child for three weeks. Jill is acting out her fears that a) she won't be a good parent, b) her kid will get out of control, or c) she will be taken advantage of if she isn't totally consistent.

In *anger-based* families, unspoken messages run something like this: the only emotion that is acceptable is fear, as long as you keep it secret. The only emotion acceptable to act on is anger, as long as you overpower others. Never let your fear show. It's a sign of weakness.

Such misuse of emotional power in a family weakens a child and causes all emotional reactions to become internalized.

Think about...

Remember the last time you acted angry.

What were you afraid of, underneath?

Question Six

What do you mean by internalized?

We carry our unspoken and often unknown emotions into our lives through a process called internalization. When we internalize something, we bring it inside and make it personal. Ridicule, criticism and harshness, especially, are internalized. If we are abused, we think it's our fault. If we are criticized, we think we have a secret flaw that makes others hate us when they get to know us. If our father was very strong, authoritative, rigid, controlling and scared us with his anger and sarcasm, we think rigidity and anger is the way to react. Remember that sarcasm is a searing of the tender flesh of a child.

If we are treated with disrespect and we think it's not fair, we become angry and want to lash out. But if we are afraid to become angry at our abusers or those who have authority over us, we squash our anger. We are afraid we will be punished. We may have heard, "If you think it's bad now, just wait. I'll show you what bad can be!" Or we may think we are bad for being angry at a parent. We turn our anger inward and become angry at ourselves. In some people, this becomes depression.

The truth is that a parent who acts out his feelings rather than expressing them in a spirit of warmth and caring is usually full of his own fear and rage. In addition, he becomes secretly ashamed of his behavior. As children, we swallow what we can't say and we think the feelings are our own. We believe the things we are told: that we are bad, worthless, wrong, stupid and dumb. Our power becomes enclosed in a fist much like our parent's fist. We need to remove these feelings of fear, rage and shame from ourselves and return them to our parents. Sometimes just recognizing this fact will help to sort out our parents' problems from our own.

Think about...

What shame do you carry for your parents?

What are or were they ashamed of?

What do you have to do to return it to them?

Question Seven

I seem to have spent my whole life being afraid that no one would love me. What happened in my family to cause such absolute fear in me?

You may have come from a *fear-based* family in which there was a lot of jealousy. A fear-based family is infected with a scarcity mentality. The scarcity mentality occurs when there is not enough to go around, whether it's love, attention or pride. It is well symbolized in money and how money is handled.

Children in homes operating under the scarcity mentality feel as if whatever form of love or attention is given, they'd better hang on to, because it may never come again. Children in these homes seem to be demanding of love and attention when they grow up and never seem to get enough. They got the clear message when youngsters that there is not enough to go around. There may or may not be enough money and food and shelter in reality, but love and attention, esteem and pride in the child are at a real premium. Further, love and attention can be taken away without warning, if children do not please parents or perform, that is, behave in the ways parents deem acceptable. They feel inside, "I will never be accepted or loved if I don't do...or say...what is pleasing."

This kind of family can produce people who feel like helpless victims and see themselves as depressed. Recovering people operate out of abundancy, not scarcity.

Think about...

How did the scarcity mentality operate in your home?

How do you still keep it going?

To whom do you ration your attention and caring today?

How can you express the abundance mentality today?

Question Eight

I came from a home that seemed rather normal to me. My parents did not drink and they didn't even fight. Yet I seem to have all the symptoms of codependency.

Subtle Codependency is missed or easily explained away. The strands of codependency feel like spaghetti. They are difficult to separate and identify. This kind of codependency can manifest as depression, chronic illness, strict religion, workaholism, even TV watching. The dysfunction occurs when the feelings of people are sacrificed for something they can't believe in.

This can happen when one or more of these conditions exist:

1. When the system (family, government, work place, church) is more important than the people it was designed to serve.

2. When the system is rigid and closed-ended.

3. When there is some secret to protect.

4. When communication is blocked, unclear, ambiguous and indirect.

5. When there is a hierarchal system with one person at the top and strict rules handed down without consideration for the well-being of each and every member.

6. When there is a focus on something other than love, attention, closeness and growth between and among the members of the group.

7. When the norms of the group revolve around the whims or moods of one person rather than the well-being of all.

8. When the purpose of the group is unclear or unpredictable and it changes capriciously.

When we lose our power even in subtle ways, codependency rears its head and people are infected. We are deeply wounded. We lose our soul.

Think about...

How did you lose your power?

What happened?

How did it feel?

Was it a rigid family system or another kind of group that robbed you of your soul?

How long did it take you recognize that there was something wrong?

Question Nine

How can I recognize the signs of subtle codependency?

You can ask yourself a series of questions to determine if you've been affected: How do I control my world? Do I control internally, through withdrawal and isolation? By manipulating others (for their own good, of course)?

How do I view other people? Sometimes we call ourselves a perpetual optimist, seeing only potential for good in others. Sometimes we try to encourage others to live up to our view of their potential. Often we suffer from the Blind Spot Syndrome. That is, we see other people in *only* the best possible light. The truth is, if we see flaws in others, we may reject them because we don't know how to negotiate our love.

Do I know what my opinions are? Do I focus so much on fixing other people's lives that I am not aware of my own opinions? Have I not taken the time and energy or responsibility to form opinions of my own? Opinions are not fact.

Do I recognize and honor my feelings? Do I tune out my own feelings in an effort to be cheerful and serene for others? Do I then think I have high self-esteem, when I simply ignore my own feelings?

Am I able to do what I set out to do? To follow my own heart? Or do I have low energy to get what I want and need? Do I even *know* what I want and need?

Do I see the world in either-or terms? When seeking solutions to problems, the healthy person will look at many options and choices. As codependents, we may overuse words such as *always* and *never*.

Gray is a blend of black and white, but there is a whole spectrum of colors in a rainbow.

Think about…

If subtle codependency has gotten you, how does it show up?

Draw your feelings.

Question Ten

My husband is sarcastic to me in front of the children. Yet he gives me everything I want materially. We have a lovely home, trips, even a boat. All I do is try to make him happy and be a good wife. I think he'll be different next time but he never is. Can you help me?

This is *classic codependency*: a compliant codependent and a controlling codependent. Both are dealing with emotional survival issues.

The two of you are on a *teeter-totter*. Some people cannot become close to another but must put emotional distance between them. Your husband may be angry at his feelings of dependency and express that anger in sarcasm. He may be afraid he'll rely on you too much and be eaten up. Just when you feel most close, he pulls away.

You, on the other end of the teeter-totter, try even harder to please because you're afraid he won't love you and you'll be abandoned. You try to cajole him into loving you. The harder you try, the more he distances. The more he distances, the harder you try. Up and down you go with fear, anger and blame doing the balancing.

People on a teeter-totter need to stop, get their feet on the ground and negotiate the goals of their emotional relationship. Clearly, neither partner is happy. Relationship skills can be learned, once people break denial. There is hope.

Think about...

What one thing are you willing to change to improve your relationship?

What one thing do you feel you cannot — or must not — change in an effort to improve your relationship?

CORE ISSUES

Question Eleven

What is a core issue?

Core issues are sensitive areas about which we are touchy. They are like deep bruises on the soul. If one of these areas is touched, we will react strongly, perhaps over-react.

Each of us has a general motif underlying what we think and how we feel. A motif is made up of several dominant and recurrent themes. We become aware of our themes when we begin to say, "I seem to be living out a pattern here. Every man I fall in love with is unavailable in one way or another. He's either married, lives far away or doesn't respond to my emotional needs."

Another motif might run something like, "I shoot myself in the foot all the time. I left my last job just before someone else got the promotion I wanted." A person might hear himself saying, "I never seem to be able to finish anything. I flunked out of college when I had only one semester left to finish my degree."

Sometimes motifs are condensed into mottos such as, "If he doesn't love me, who will? I know I'm not good enough for someone to love." Often I hear my mother say, "If you can't do it right, don't do it at all." No wonder I'm such a perfectionist!

Most of our behavior is centered around a particular motif or pattern learned long ago. In psychology we call them *therapeutic issues* or *core issues*. These are emotional, rather than spiritual, issues.

Laws of spirituality are broad, abstract, non-local and transcendent. For most of us, mystical experiences transcend but do not eliminate the needs of the body, including emotional needs. Sometimes we don't differentiate between these related but separate needs.

Laws of emotions are local, specific and tied to the body. We might meditate or pray about something and know that spiritually we are on the right track. But then our body, with its innate wisdom, tells us that there is still an emotional issue to deal with. If we ignore our body and its messages, we may become confused and discouraged. Our soul can get caught in our emotional traps. Our soul seems to lie under the trap. We must clear out our emotional debris to free our soul. Then our core will be clear and open to receive the Spirit or God.

The core of an apple is what holds the apple together. If the core is soft or spoiled, it will be filled with decaying material and eventually the apple will show bruises. The work of recovery lies in unearthing and healing these core issues so that the apple can be round, ripe and delicious to our taste.

Think about...

In one sentence or phrase, write your general motif and themes that keep you from getting what you want out of life.

Name two instances in your experience when your body told you that there was an emotional issue with which you needed to deal.

DENIAL

Question Twelve

What is denial?

Denial is a natural human response to conditions we cannot afford to face or to feel. It begins when we are children in unhealthy homes. It is our way of protecting ourselves. It is an unconscious process necessary for survival under certain conditions. For example, if as children, we depend on our mother to survive but she hurts us, we must deny this reality. We must deny that we feel afraid, angry or hurt. The problem is that denial does not end with childhood. As adults we keep re-enacting our childhood until we come to terms with our pain. The exact situation may be different, but our emotional quality of life remains the same.

I once had a beautiful, colorful puffer fish. I put it in my tank and it ate all the other fish. It was still very beautiful, swimming all alone in the empty tank. I missed my other fish.

Denial, like the puffer fish, is a very strong survivor. Codependent patterns seem to work for a very long time. But what really may be working is denial. Denial occurs when there is too much to lose in looking under the surface.

Things can look good on the outside but if there is a waking shadow under the surface, we need to bring it up to the light of day.

When I say that denial is strong, I mean that its strength comes from the fact that it is unconscious. It is a wall that cannot be broken or even dented until it is made conscious. Awareness opens our eyes. Then we see what we could not afford to see earlier. We feel what we could not afford to feel. We are able to tell the truth.

Telling the truth means facing the consequences of our actions. It means stopping a negative activity or attitude which may be paying off for us in some way. It means taking initiative to create new actions to replace those that aren't working. This feels very risky to us.

We build walls to defend ourselves against others instead of bridges to cross over to them. Denial wears many faces. Many of them are hidden in the individual and in society. Denial makes possible the impossible and credible the incredible.

Think about…

How might you be using denial to protect yourself now?

What would you risk if you broke denial right now?

Question Thirteen

Is denial always negative?

Denial is not always negative in itself. There is positive denial which enables us to act in extraordinary ways and to deny facts we cannot control. An example of positive denial is found in those suffering terminal illness, who have fought and won a battle for life because they believed they could. It occurs in each of us when we live each day as if we were never to die. Aeronautically, the bumblebee cannot fly. Its body is too heavy for its small, light wings. But the bumblebee doesn't know this, so it flies anyway. And we often do the same.

Think about...

Can you find an example of how positive denial works in your life today?

WHO IT AFFECTS

Question Fourteen

Is codependency different for men and women?

There are important gender differences that must be recognized and worked with. Codependency will show itself in women in different ways from its manifestations in men.

In a codependent relationship without alcohol, a woman may do more for a man to show her love than he does for her, so she may appear to be acting more codependently. Her focus is on him, his comfort and his desires. She may give up her friends and her activities for him and his friends and his activities. She may say things like, "Because I love you, I want to please you in all ways."

It doesn't matter to her what they are doing, as long as they are together. She may send loving cards and write little notes. She is very open about her feelings and tries to build closeness, so she won't be abandoned.

A man in the same relationship, however, may unconsciously give a woman power in other ways. He may be afraid of rejection. While he may not do as much for her emotionally or in physical comfort, he cares to excess about her opinion of him. He desperately needs her approval. Because he has been conditioned not to show his feelings, he may not express his feelings to her. He may even take the opposite approach and deny those feelings.

At the same time, he may be overly sensitive to criticism from her and may even perceive critical behavior where there is none.

So she openly shows her dependence or focus on him. He closets his. At bottom, they are both afraid of abandonment, whether it is called that or rejection. They are both codependent.

Think about...

How has codependency affected you in your current or most recent female/male relationship?

Question Fifteen

How does codependency show up in lesbian or gay relationships? I'm afraid to commit to a love relationship, yet I desperately want one.

It is not sexual preference that causes trouble in such relationships. It is the inequality of power and control of vital resources such as love, sex, money that creates codependency. Perception of inequality is the same thing as real inequality. Even if one person *feels* the inequality, it is a set-up for codependent reactions.

One person may have learned helplessness while the partner rescues, makes the decisions and consequently feels put upon. The helpless one stays shamed because she does not experience her own power or control over her life. Resentments grow between them as mutual codependency flourishes. This is no different from the codependent dynamics in a heterosexual relationship.

Gay or straight, codependents sometimes make an early decision not to be in a relationship with anyone, thinking that will keep them safe. Not becoming involved is another face of codependency. It is fear of intimacy which keeps us isolated from one another.

We need to learn the dance of intimacy, to come close together in loving harmonious relationship and then to separate when the need arises. Learning to balance the need for intimacy, closeness and relatedness with the equally strong and equally valid need for autonomy, independent thinking and time to be alone is a major task of recovery and of life. The arms of fear can't hold you close, can't keep you warm, can't shelter your heart.

Think about…

When you hear the word intimacy, how do you feel?

What picture do you get?

In what ways is your relationship unequal?

When you begin to feel close to or intimate with someone, what do you do?

When you think of the word intimacy, what picture do you get?

Question Sixteen

Can codependency exist in non-sexual, same-sex relationships?

Yes. The seeds of codependency begin with an unequal relationship, one in which one person has more power than the other. The power is off-balance when the relationship begins.

Relationships which begin with inequality are mentor-employee, teacher-student, supervisor-supervisee, sponsor-sponsee. What begins as a sincere effort to help and teach and a sincere willingness and openness to learn, may turn into a nightmare of codependency.

It can also occur in roommates. We saw this in the TV show, *The Odd Couple*. One person may have signed a lease while the other assumes no legal responsibility. One roommate may be willing to talk through difficulties while the other clams up. One of the two pays the bills on time but the other does not. One does his share of housekeeping while the other consistently procrastinates. *Then the fights begin.*

It can also occur in friendships in which one person "always" comes to the other for help and counseling; and the other "always" listens. Codependency turns responsibility into fear and caring into anger.

Think about…

Which of your current same-sex, non-sexual relationships are unequal in power?

How does codependency show itself in these relationships?

When you think of breaking a codependent relationship, what do you have to lose?

Question Seventeen

I don't want this to happen. What are the signs I should look for?

Codependency begins with mutual attraction. But it begins un-equally, with one person giving more and the other taking more. It is usually not two givers who are involved, but a giver and a taker. The relationship may do very well as long as the needy person is in trouble and asking for or taking help, the person with lower status stays in that position or the student stays a student and doesn't graduate or outstrip the teacher. Remember that the beginning is inequality of *power* with no mechanism to balance that power.

Where there are unclear, ambiguous expectations between the two and a lack of effective communication about the relationship, the possibility for trouble exists. Where either or both people are secretly afraid of abandonment, need to be depended upon or manipulate instead of negotiate, there will surely be a problem. Playing dumb or innocent, one person refusing to take responsi-bility for his part, blaming the person in power for what happens in the relationship and placating behavior followed by anger are sure set-ups for codependent reactions. Clear and well-defined boundaries are vital to a relationship. Where one or both people have poor and undefined boundaries or rigid ones, there will be overstepping boundaries that should have been defined. A mecha-nism for handling potential conflict must be set up.

Once the patient gets better, the student graduates or the employee is promoted, the relationship must shift dramatically. The balance of power and authority must be equalized by both parties. This is difficult to do once habits of relating have been formed. The dynamics seem comfortable for both people because they are familiar. We mistake familiarity for comfort. We are used to dealing with the imbalance of power that we saw in our compliant/controller homes.

Think about…

Do you have any of these kinds of professional codependency relationships?

If so, how did it get started?

Where is it now?

HOW IT AFFECTS US

Question Eighteen

I hear the voice of my father every time I fail at something, especially in business. He was very critical and judgmental but he has been dead for a very long time. I was not aware of this until my wife pointed out that every time I am to do something in business that would create success, I seem to sabotage myself and stop my success. We talked about it, and it was then that I identified what my father said to me, about me, about the world and about himself. I began to listen closely to the talk that goes on inside my head. "Those people get all the breaks." "That's not for the likes of you, boy!" "Who do you think you are, some fancy pants?" "You can't even throw a ball right. You throw like a girl." I also don't have any friends and I tend to be a loner. I didn't think I had symptoms of codependency. But now I wonder.

Codependency is a strange condition. It goes on in our heads fully as much as in our behavior. You may be codependent with your father, even though he is dead. You seem to use your father as a referent for every (business) situation and to measure yourself against him or his values or his judgments.

Remember that codependency is a focus on a person, place or something *outside of ourselves*. This works even if the person is dead or the idea exists only in our heads or memories.

You also said you're an isolated person, having no friends. It may be that you have not learned how to interact with other people in any nourishing way. Isolation is a major feature of codependency. In actuality, it is a red flag or a signal. We can tell if we're having a codependency attack when we begin to separate ourselves either in actuality or in our minds from friends, family and even from our usual activities. We may rationalize and say things like: "I just don't feel like going out." "I really don't feel like facing people." "It feels as if there's a wall of glass between

other people and me. I can see them but I can't touch them."
"Nothing really ever touches me inside."

When that happens, we know we're in codependent trouble. If you use your father's voice to determine or judge your thinking and behavior, he becomes a check point for you. If the messages he gave were critical, judgmental or otherwise negative, you will re-experience that parent, even though the man himself is dead. Remember the line from *I Never Sang for my Father* that goes: "Death ends a life, but it does not end a relationship, which struggles on in the survivor's mind toward some final resolution, some clear meaning..."

Think about...

What lessons did your father teach you?

What were his favorite sayings?

What effect has this had on your values?

Question Nineteen

What do you mean by using my father as a "referent"?

We all have in our memories, whether we are aware of it or not, certain people who have greatly influenced our lives in our thinking, feeling or behavior. We refer to them for direction, like an internal road map. There are parents, grandparents, brothers and sisters, other relatives, friends, friends of friends, parents of friends, teachers, clergy and others. Of all these people, only certain ones have made a lasting impression. We all have those "I'll never forget... in sixth grade..." (We also have those we'd *like* to forget!)

As children, if we are in a healthy environment, we make use of those people who have something we want, though we may not be conscious of this process. It may be one person's friendly smile, another's intellectual curiosity, Aunt Ethel's tenacity. (She always got what she wanted, it was said).

We learn from books, magazines, TV and newspapers as well as from the ideas of our historical times. Some of us will remember the depression mentality of our parents or grandparents. It seems as if they never got over their experience of the Great Depression.

We unconsciously group these people, ideas and qualities together to form an internal map. This reference group becomes part of the criteria or standards for our behavior because we constantly refer to them. Throughout life, we use these standards to measure our actions and even our thoughts. We often verbalize, "My father always said..." or "Mother said..."

We also use measuring sticks that are largely unconscious. This occurs when we find ourselves thinking or acting like one of our parents. If we verbalized how that happened, we might say, "My mother thought..." as if we knew what Mother thought or felt.

A problem in unhealthy, restricted homes is that our natural capacity for growing through association with and imitation of others is not encouraged. And our ability to take in healthy qualities is frustrated, inhibited or warped.

If you use your "father's voice" to determine or judge your thinking and behavior, he is running your life. If you "hear" conflicting voices from different referents, you may be constantly fighting battles inside yourself and really not know who you are.

Think about…

Who were the people who influenced your life the most?

How did they form your value system?

Name two areas of your life in which you most often hear referent's voices.

Question Twenty

My Dad has been in Alcoholics Anonymous for ten years. Even though he doesn't drink, he still seems unreasonable and rigid. He still tries to control my life and tell me what to do. He has not changed. Why is this? Doesn't AA work?

AA does what it was designed to do. It keeps a person from drinking. But there is a phenomenon called *dry drunk*, which occurs when a person no longer drinks alcohol, but has not been treated for the underlying codependent issues.

Dry drunk means that a person does not drink alcohol or use other drugs, but periodically tissue needs build up toxins in the body and he acts as *if* he is drunk or has been drinking.

Alcoholism seems to be a disease of anger, whether or not the accompanying codependency is treated. Unresolved rage may lie in the tissues and cells of a person for years until it is released by a chemical reaction of some kind and erupts as a full blown temper tantrum. When a person has become addicted to alcohol, the body remembers the rage at a cellular level and remembers the release of the rage through alcohol. Although alcohol is no longer used, the reaction remains.

Think about...

When you hear the term, "alcoholism as a disease" inside, how do you feel?

Why?

Question Twenty-One

My mother is mad at me again. She won't talk to me. This happens all the time. It's because I talked to my sister and told her what I thought about what Mom did to us when we were children. I told my sister not to say anything. But she had to go and tell Mom and now Mom won't speak to me. Can you help?

This is a common pattern in dysfunctional families. It has to do with a major flaw in some families: poor communication skills resulting in *triangulation*. A good scenario runs something like this: Dad says to Mom, "Your son David is a lazy slob. Tell him he'd better do some work around here for a change. I have to do it all! I work hard all day and the work is never done." A triangle is formed: Dad, Mom, David.

Dad may rant and rave at Mom about David, but he doesn't talk to David directly. What has been accomplished here is that Dad has avoided direct encounter with David. He has laid the responsibility on Mom. Mom is enabling the behavior and if she does tell David, she has put herself between two people she loves. David has avoided a direct encounter or confrontation with his father and can blame his father and see him as an ogre, always giving orders.

The family system goes round and round. David may never really mow the lawn. And he learns to create chaos to avoid responsibility. If he does mow the lawn, he can bitterly resent it and his father and often he will blame his mother also. He learns to blame and shame others for his part of responsibility to the family.

In the above scenario, all members of the family get hurt and end up feeling bad, shamed and blamed. Father feels bad because he yelled at his wife for something that was not her fault. He also may feel ashamed because he doesn't go directly to his son with the issue. Mother feels bad because Father yelled at her and now because she has to deliver an unpleasant message to her child. She also feels ashamed because she can't tell Father, "Why not tell David directly how you feel, John?" and walk away. The son feels bad because he does not have a chance to speak directly to Father who is giving the orders and he does not have a chance either to tell his side or negotiate. Here's what usually happens:

The first communication is from Dad to Mom. "Tell David ..." Now Mom has the ball. Dad effectively tells Mom he's over-worked, blames David, is critical of David, avoids a direct encounter with his son, gives an unclear message as to the specific job he wants done, and he delegates Mom to communicate all of this to son. Now Dad is off the hook

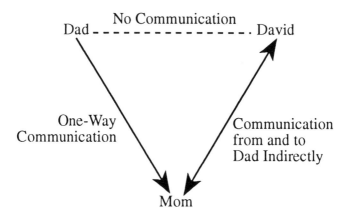

Second communication is between Mom and David. Mom gets between Dad and David. David now avoids direct contact with his father, feels guilty because Mom is involved, doesn't know exactly what job he is to do and when, is ashamed because his father works so hard, and somehow feels it is his (David's) fault, and ends up resenting both his father and his mother.

The third communication is between David and Mom. David gets to tell Mom just what he thinks of his father. Now Mom feels bad about the poor relationship between two people she loves.

Nothing gets resolved!

Triangles are about getting another person to change. They are about defocusing the attention from our behavior. They are about giving unclear and indirect messages to others and then blaming them for not understanding. They are about avoiding responsibility for our part in our family relationships.

The function of triangles is to keep the status quo in the unhealthy family system, to avoid solving the problems. Like other forms of gossip, we make ourselves look good by blaming and shaming others.

Awareness of triangulating is crucial to recovery.

Think about...

How do triangles work in your family?

Work group?

Friendships?

How do you keep them going?

Put in your own names in the triangle.

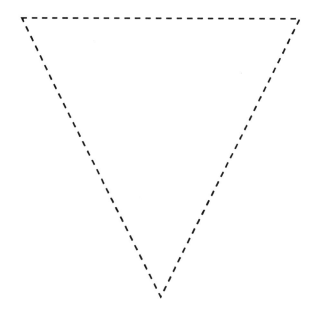

Question Twenty-Two

In my family, no one minds their own business. If I have a problem at work, sure as shootin', everyone in the family knows about it before morning. What is this all about anyway?

Inside a family, several forces work to keep the system going and to keep people imprisoned. One of these forces is called boundaries. Boundaries are on a continuum, ranging from no boundaries to rigid boundaries.

The acting out of these boundaries results in a pattern that could look like this:

Emotional Emotional Emotional
Enmeshment ←→ Flexibility ←→ Isolation

Boundaries are physical, emotional, social, intellectual and spiritual ways that keep us whole. They prevent our lives from being absorbed by other people. They keep us from absorbing others also. Boundaries keep our souls from disappearing when our power leaks out. Boundaries are not unlike borders of countries.

When we have had unpredictable parents who loved in one mood and rejected in another, with our having no way of knowing which will be presented to us, our boundaries blur, blend or break. Physical, emotional and sexual abuse violates our boundaries. It intrudes into our inner space and leaves wounds and scars. It abuses our souls. Often this wounding is done in the false name of love. And our love is abused.

As adults, we may get close to another person and become frightened of the vulnerability of closeness and then veer away. We may overcompensate. Or we may become so involved in other people's affairs that there is no separate space between us.

Boundaries can be *internal* or *external*. Internal boundaries allow us to make good decisions, based on our own best interests. With good boundaries, we take responsibility for our own actions and we set reasonable *limits* on the actions of others.

External boundaries allow us to choose distances from others that are appropriate and realistic, based again, on our best interests. Good external boundaries keep us emotionally close to others in safe, comfortable ways.

It sounds like your family is enmeshed. You may need outside help to sort this out.

Think about...

An example from your own life of physical boundaries...

...emotional boundaries

...social boundaries

...mind boundaries

Question Twenty-Three

When I was in high school, I remember doing well in academics and in sports. One night I was doing homework in my room and my mother walked in. She said, "What are you doing, still studying? A young girl like you should be out with boys and doing fun things." I tried to be a good girl and to please mother.

So the next year, I had fun. My grades went down to C's (never D's) and I went out with my friends a lot. Then one night when I came home at 12:15 instead of 12:00, my mother met me at the door and said, "You should be ashamed of yourself. You are not doing that well in school and here you are, running around all night long with who knows who! You should be studying!" Damned if I do and damned if I don't. I now find it difficult, if not sometimes impossible, as an adult, to make decisions. No matter what I do, I think I should have done something else. No matter how I act, I am ashamed of myself and feel terrible about myself. I'm afraid to do anything now.

We teach our children to have no confidence, to be poor decision-makers, to depend on others for approval. A child's concept of herself is based on parental approval. If the child is criticized for doing what she thinks a parent wants her to, she becomes confused by the criticism. When the child then switches to another action and still does not please her parent, she becomes even more confused. The predicament you describe is a classic *double bind* situation. This means that only two choices are presented and neither one is viable. The child cannot gain approval no matter which decision she makes. She then feels powerless and becomes helpless to move. She caught in a vise that tightens with every word:

Don't study so hard. Have more fun.
OK, I will go out more.
No, that's wrong.
You want me to stay home more?

No. Guess again.
Tell me what you want me to do.
By now you should *know* what I expect.!
I'm trying to be a good girl. But I'm not sure what you want this time.
Why can't you ever make it easy for me?
I'm trying to make you happy. Is this what you want?
You disappointed me again! You'll *never* get it, will you.
No matter what I do, I'm wrong. I feel small, helpless, unable to move.
Oh, for heavens sake, girl! Why can't you ever make up your mind?
I feel shamed, worthless, paralyzed.

The child has *no* choice but to feel uncertainty, shame, guilt, fear and anger. And self doubt walks in to stay.

If we stay home and study, we are not loved because we are not out playing. If, on the other hand, we go out to play, we are not loved because we don't study. The unspoken Mothermessage is, "No matter what you do, *you* are not *good enough* for me!"

The truth is, the parent actually fears the future and is full of conflicts. She then projects her fear onto the child. The soul of the child shudders and shuts its eyes.

Think about...

What is your current bind?

What was it as a kid?

Draw your own vise.

Question Twenty-Four

What is a double bind?

A double bind is a situation in which, no matter what you do or which way you turn, you lose. It is a set-up. At best, you are in trouble. At worst, you lose everything. Usually a person is presented with two choices, neither of which will be acceptable. This is often presented in small ways. It is your job to fix dinner. If you fix roast beef, the message is, "Don't you know that beef isn't good for me?" If you fix a vegetable dish, it's, "I am sick and tired of weak, tasteless vegetables. I'd really like a good steak!" You're in a vise!

But double messages are also created in a family when we are given the clear but unspoken message that runs something like this:

"Now, listen to me. I'm going to give you a job to do. It is the most important job in your life. In fact, it is a job that will save or destroy our family and me. But I'm not going to tell you exactly what that job is. You will just have to guess from my behavior and non-verbal clues what the job is. Not only that, but I will not give you any tools you need to do that job. Remember that it is an extremely important and vital job and only you can do it. Also, it must be done exactly *right* — or all will be lost. Don't ask any questions now!

"In addition, listen to me now! If you can't do the job *exactly* right and you *fail*, something terrible, something dire will happen and it will be *all your fault*. But I'm not going to tell you *what* will happen. Now, hurry up and do the job, because time is running out fast."

When as young children, we are given such a situation, it doesn't matter what we do. We will not be allowed to save the situation even though we are programmed to do so, because what is happening here is that there is a dysfunctional, codependent family (who may be alcoholic but not always) which perceives itself to be in constant crisis and is badly in need of repair. But none of the adults is willing to make any changes. So the chaos and crisis goes on and on and on, no matter what the child does.

And the message repeats itself in our unconscious for years.

Think about...

Who puts you in the double bind?

How do you stay there?

Draw your double binds.

Question Twenty-Five

You mean I have to carry the double bind of my childhood into my current life?

Yes, unless we change it. When we grow up, we seem to be drawn like a magnet to needy, crisis-ridden people and situations. The child, now adult, repeats the patterns learned at home. Something is terribly wrong. Constant crises appear. And it is up to *me* to fix it all. Or something terrible will happen and it will be *all my fault*. There is no thinking in this situation. There is only reacting, like the child we were. We may even be *addicted to the drama* of it all, even though there is a desperation beneath the excitement.

An example from the work place shows an office that is extremely busy and there is an inordinate amount of work to do for each person. The company has a policy of keeping one less employee than is needed to do the job. This results in each person, in addition to doing his own job, taking on some extra tasks from the job that has no person assigned to it. In any group of people, there will be some who will not do any more than their own job, and some who do not even do their own job. So the slack falls to the now-codependent Adult Child who has learned to handle it all. The codependent will fix it for the entire group, *no matter what the cost.*

As an Adult Child codependent, we work and work extra hours for little pay, get no rewards and stress ourselves out to the max, with little results. We have learned not to go to authority for help, so we say nothing. Here's what happens: we feel like dirt, shamed, less-than, inadequate. We get confused and try to cloud the issue. We resent being confused because it doesn't work. So, we become angrier and angrier and angrier until we blow up and quit without saying anything or we become passive-aggressive and take lots of days off from work. We either get physically sick or we numb out to the point where we function in a robot-like manner. We have no energy for anything in life but work. And we get burned-out and *no one even notices that we are dying.* Just as it was when we were children.

Think about...

Are you in a double bind today?

Explain or draw it.

Question Twenty-Six

How do I get out of a double bind?

A child cannot get out of a double bind. A child has no authority, no mobility, no choices.

For adults to get out of a double bind, we must be willing to take an emotional risk. We must be willing to face the consequences of our actions. We must be willing to go to the mat. We must give up the approval of others, even the approval of ourselves at first.

We don't take the impossible job and we don't go to extremes. We don't respond to unclear messages. We clarify our own position and ask for clear and simple directions. We ask objectively how our performance is measured. We give up other people's authority and use our own. We take our own power back. We recall our souls.

Think about...

How do you feel when you get into a bind like this?

How do you unbind?

Question Twenty-Seven

How can I do this? I don't even know where to begin.

Begin by making a list of your "shoulds" and examine them one by one. Some of your shoulds are good and you may want to keep them: "I should get more exercise." Others are harmful: "You'll never amount to anything. You ought to be ashamed of yourself." The ones you decide are not in your own best interests, you must abandon.

At the same time, do affirmations every day, three times a day. Shoulds and affirmations are different. Shoulds are externally originated. They are the prescriptions (rules and regulations: what to do) and proscriptions (prohibitions and judgments: what not to do) of others. Our society, through institutions such as family, church, schools and work-places, prescribes and proscribes not only behavior, but attitudes, beliefs and values. An attitudinal *prescription* tells us that we must respect *all* authority. A belief *prescription* holds that one must go to church every Sunday. A value *proscription* says one must never go against what his family thinks is right.

Within the bounds of common sense (or what it takes for a society to function), we have not only a right, but an obligation to change what isn't working well. So we can and *should* change some "shoulds". The decision about which rules and prohibitions we need to change is based on our individual priorities.

Some shoulds are used by our institutions as a means of social control and others are used as a means of personal power over others. It is healthy to question the laws handed down to us when they don't seem to fit our experience. That's what political lobbying is about.

On the personal level, it is healthy to question the prescriptions and proscriptions handed down to us by our families. Our "shoulds" are a form of training or regulating our behavior, thinking and feeling. Our "shoulds" become our internal "program". We often believe that we are no more than our shoulds. But a harmful program can and must be changed.

Affirmations, on the other hand, are created by a healthy person as a way of changing societal or institutional programming that is no longer appropriate, realistic or meaningful. Affirmations *should* reflect how you choose to act, think or feel. Affirmations are a vital part of healing. They are a verbal way to bind our wounds and to ease our pain. Affirmations replace sickness with health and despair with hope. When we create and use affirmations in our healing, we assert that something is true. We confirm our own decisions. We become self-determining adults.

Affirmations must be done one at a time, using short, simple phrases or sentences. There are many good books on Affirmations. Pick out two or three that fit you and your situation. Or make up your own.

You must begin with a very relaxed state of BodyMindSoul. The new thoughts must be repeated many times. As we move the old voices out of the way, we begin to hear the truth. We begin to tell the truth to ourselves. We begin the story of our own lives. And we sing our own songs.

Think about...

One of my favorite affirmations is: As I grow, everyone grows. Write three affirmations for yourself. Practice them daily while in a relaxed state.

1.

2.

3.

Question Twenty-Eight

I don't feel at all connected to my family. I just don't seem to feel close to them. I never did. What's wrong with me?

A process that reduces power in a child within a family has to do with faulty *bonding*.

In humans, there is a natural symbiotic relationship between mother and infant. In the time before birth, they share the same life through the umbilical cord. When the child is born, mother and infant fall in love and bond. The birth bonding is necessary for psychological health and physical well-being of both and insures survival.

In a healthy system, both mother and child have enough experiences together to feel *safe* with each other. As the child grows there is a natural, spontaneous separation process that is part of the development of both mother and child. There is a natural loosening of the common life of the two. The healthy process allows them to be two whole people.

THE BONDING PROCESS

Before birth, mother and child have one common life and are intertwined in a biological process called symbiosis.

Mother and child Symbiosis: same life
before birth

When the child is born, there is a natural dependency, each on the other. Mother needs child to empty breasts and return womb to pre-pregnancy condition. Child needs mother to survive. The child feels no separation, only oneness and connection.

Child is born Natural interdependency
between mother and child

As the child grows, there is a natural letting-go, separation process that occurs in regular, orderly stages. This becomes psychological as well as biological as the child grows older.

Development
of child Progression of
growth and
Psychological
separation

Finally, the two are separate, unique individuals, with lives of their own. They may remain close or not, but whatever happens with the mother-of-origin, the child-become-adult transfers his experiences to a significant other. If his early experiences have been positive, he will form healthy relationships. If not, he becomes codependent — or worse.

Individuation  Closeness
Independence

Interdependence

In adulthood, bonding occurs in any significant, deeply moving relationship. We feel bonded with parents, brothers and sisters, friends and lovers.

A bond is something that holds two people together and commits them to caring. A bond is created through connection. It can be a physical bond like that of mother and child or a sexual bond, like that between lovers. Strong bonding is necessary for emotional survival and growth. In a dangerous or potentially dangerous situation, a healthy bonding process creates a physical, emotional or psychological safety zone.

For bonding to occur, there must be a mutual exchange of energy on a significant level — physical, emotional, sexual, spiritual. The exchange of energy creates the glue for the bonding. The more levels that are involved, the deeper the bonds.

In faulty bonding, the tendency is toward isolation or enmeshment. Emotional isolation occurs when a baby is not allowed to bond in a natural way. If a parent or surrogate cannot become or cannot stay close to a child, if separation occurs too early in life, if the baby is not handled enough or is handled in a rough way, the child will not feel safe enough to bond. If, when a child comes close physically or emotionally, it is hurt, it will become more and more isolated.

Emotional enmeshment occurs when a baby is not allowed to separate at the appropriate time. If a parent or surrogate is overprotective and will not let go to allow the child to become an independent person, the child will not bond properly and will try to move away.

What most often happens, is inconsistent parenting in which there is a push-pull dynamic in the mother-child relationship. A child who is so bonded will pull away when he feels too close and draw the other person closer when he feels too distant, regardless of the needs of the other person. He does not know how to do the dance of intimacy.

Think about...

How does bonding work in your present relationship?

When do you feel the closest?

The most distant?

How do you avoid closeness?

Did you have faulty or incomplete bonding as a child?

How did this happen?

Question Twenty-Nine

I feel bonded with my boyfriend, even though I know he isn't good for me. What can I do?

There is *healthy* bonding through pleasure, love and joy in an atmosphere of safety, commitment and caring. There is *unhealthy* bonding through pain, fear and anger in an atmosphere of abuse, unavailability and possessiveness.

Healthy bonding feels safe. Unhealthy bonding feels dangerous.

You need to determine whether your inner feelings include pain, fear and anger — or safety, commitment and caring. You need to listen to your body when you are not with him, to discriminate between purely sexual feelings and those of safety, commitment and caring. Sexual feelings are strong and tend to sweep us away with their power. But under the sexual feelings there often lies a fearful, small child.

A child who cannot bond or cannot separate becomes confused about closeness in relationships. As an adult, that child learns to ignore, neglect, mistreat and otherwise abuse her Inner Child. She will then have great difficulty choosing healthy people to be around. The Inner Child is a concept that stands for our emotions and our childhood memories. See Question Thirty-Six for further treatment of this idea. If this seems to fit, you may need help to sort out your feelings.

Think about...

What's an example of unhealthy bonding in your life?

What in your childhood does it remind you of?

CHARACTERISTICS OF CODEPENDENTS

Question Thirty

I have heard that codependents are overly responsible for others. I am not like that at all. I'm often the last one to offer favors to others. Can I still be codependent?

Yes. Under-responsibility is the polar opposite of over-responsibility. It is part of the codependent condition. What this means is that there are two extremes of behavior and codependents tend to be at one end or the other. A person in a relationship will often exhibit both over and under responsibility, veering from one extreme to the other. Depending on the relationship, a codependent will also take on the opposite role of a significant other, thus filling a perceived emotional gap.

Or a person will not become involved at all, thinking that non-involvement is a guarantee of emotional safety.

Recovery lies in the balance between taking care of ourselves and serving others. Whether you are at the North Pole or the South Pole, you will still freeze and die.

Think about...

In what areas of your life are you most extreme?

Recall times when you were over-responsible?

How did you feel?

Recall times when you were under-responsible?

How did you feel?

Question Thirty-One

One of the things I've heard about codependents is that we are afraid of authority figures. Does this mean police officers, teachers, clergy and others who have some kind of legal or moral power over us? I seem to also be shy or inhibited with grocery clerks and co-workers. Why is this?

When we say that codependents are afraid of authority figures, we mean that *when* we are suffering the symptoms of codependency, we revert back to our childhood ways.

Codependency has been described as a failure to complete developmental tasks. We often do not develop our own values, attitudes and beliefs as adults in an adult world. We print when we need to learn to write. As St. Paul says, "When I was a child, I thought as a child; I felt as a child; I ..."

A child will *either* follow the rules of his parents or he will rebel against them. He will *react* rather than *act* for himself. If our Inner Child is insecure and unsure, as adults we may look for new parents. We seek people either to tell us what to do or to rebel against.

To an Adult Child authority means an originator, a powerful, god-like figure. An authority has the *power* to make and enforce rules and to determine or judge behavior. When we grow up, we *re-evaluate* what we have learned as children. We are called "Adult Children" because we *look* like an adult but *feel* like a child. Thus *everyone* becomes more powerful than we. *Everyone* becomes the expert. *Everyone* becomes the parent, the God. And we remain the child until we decide to become our own parent, our own authority. Then we empower ourselves to create our own experience. We can hold our own life as we hold our own Inner Child.

Think about...

Who are your authority figures?

How could you begin to stop giving others your power?

To whom do you give the power to judge your behavior?

Question Thirty-Two

I seem to hate myself and no matter what I do, I'm never satisfied or pleased with myself. Do all codependents have low self-esteem?

Usually, but not always. If we have been raised in ways that disempower us, we often feel helpless and unable to change. We may be outwardly successful but inwardly, emotionally, we are like little children. Often what we feel on the inside doesn't match what we show on the outside. We learn ways to hide our feelings from others and most especially from ourselves. We become emotionally empty. We feel deprived and starved. Then we take it out on ourselves, often through our physical or psychological symptoms.

Self-esteem can be different in various areas of our lives. Perhaps we are confident in our ability to solve problems. We may like ourselves in this area to a great degree. In an emotional situation however, we may feel utterly inept. We have no experience with emotions.

In general, to hold someone in high esteem means to place a high value on, to respect, to prize. We say recovery is falling in love with yourself, not in any self-absorbed or self-centered way, but in a simple way, like a child.

A child naturally looks to others for his self-esteem. Our self-esteem grows in direct proportion to the respect and value placed on us by our parents. The value and respect our parents have for themselves and for each other is where the esteem issue begins. If we are considered a burden to our parents, we will be a burden to ourselves. If guilt and shame were used as a means of controlling us, we will feel guilty and become ashamed of *ourselves*.

Add to this our innate capacity for picking up the shame, guilt and fears of others and making them our own. We become a child with low self-esteem, who "hates myself, no matter what I do." Self-confidence grows out of self-esteem.

We see ourselves reflected in the mirror of our parent's face. What we see there is what we become. If the parent-mirror reflects envy, dislike, anger, fear, we will internalize these as *our own*. If, on the other hand, we look into the parent eyes and see approval, encouragement, genuine love and respect, we internalize these as our own also. Further, we experience our feelings as *me*, even though we cannot label them.

As children, we are totally *in* our own experience. It is all we have. We are in the present moment at all times. Until we gain some physical, intellectual and emotional maturity, we absorb and reflect our environment. We see our image on the faces of the parents who look at us. A look can stab a soul. A hug can soothe a hurt. And a soul can return.

Think about…

In what specific areas do you feel a lack of self-esteem?

Is self-esteem different for you than self-confidence?

In what specific areas do you feel self-confident?

How was your self-esteem built?

PART TWO

Psychological Processes

Inner Child

Processes

PSYCHOLOGICAL PROCESSES

In Part One we examined some of the ways in which we have lost our power within a family system. This creates disempowerment, which brings an inner devastation. We are unable to change our world or our fate. We do not feel our inner strength, nor do we see ourselves as potent. Since we feel impotent, we seldom live out our potential. We may be outwardly successful, but inwardly, emotionally, we feel as powerless and helpless as children. The synonym Adult Children has come from this dichotomy.

Often our insides don't match our outsides. We learn ways to hide our helplessness from others and most especially from ourselves. Our shame becomes more deeply buried. The child that we once were, our Inner Child, lies hidden in the depths of our being. We become emotionally empty. We feel deprived and starved. No matter how much we eat, we are never full. We have lost our soul.

After a time, we vaguely sense that we re-enact the emotional drama of our childhood. We live out the old scripts of our lives. We become less of ourselves as we put on masks of dishonesty, secrecy and apathy to hide our shame and our helplessness.

As our mirrors reflect to us our false images, we become terrified and isolated behind our masks. And we become less alive. Our own drama takes form and plays out in the power arenas of our lives. We experience and express our disempowerment through the ongoing psychological processes called codependency.

PROCESSES: THE INNER CHILD

Question Thirty-Three

What are some signs of codependency? Of a mistreated Inner Child?

Signs and symptoms of codependency show up when we begin to react in rigid ways. We experience either emotional flooding *or* emotional paralysis.

If we are emotionally flooding, we are engulfed by feelings. We are angry and afraid all the time. We have little energy and no tolerance for mistakes, ours or those of others. We feel out of control. We feel tense and anxious and can't sleep because we feel wired. We can't make changes happen no matter how fast we run. We are running out of life and we can't stop it.

If we are emotionally paralyzed, we can't seem to feel anything at all, except depressed. Down. Out of steam. A cloud of grayness covers every day. Sometimes we feel the block in our throat, chest or stomach. We can't cope with any frustration and the smallest problem is beyond our ability to handle. We can't make decisions. We feel trapped in relationships and stuck with certain behaviors.

There is no soul in what we do or how we feel. Soulloss has sucked out our life and our power, leaving only a rigid shell of the person we were before the bloodletting.

Think about...

Have you experienced emotional flooding? What happened?

How did you feel?

What is your experience like of emotional paralysis?

How did you feel?

Question Thirty-Four

What I don't understand is why I look like an adult but feel like a child all the time. Help!

Codependency is a failure in individuation, in becoming an individual apart from our family. For a little child, attachment is safety and separation is not safe. In an atmosphere of safety, security and respect in a healthy home, a child can naturally pull away from parents to become an individual and her own person with her own identity. In this way, she learns new things and often they are things parents can't teach her. When she becomes frightened of too much space, she can move closer and know she will be totally accepted in both places. She is learning the dance of development.

In homes where there is no safety and no security, and abuse replaces respect, a child will be terrified to separate at the natural time. Or a child will not be able to bond at all. The child begins to live in the extremes. She learns either to be extremely close and enmeshed or to push away what she wants the most.

While you have developed intellectually as a competent adult, your feelings have remained behind in childhood. You have left behind a part of your soul.

Think about…

Where do you feel safe?

How can you retrieve that piece of your soul you left behind?

Question Thirty-Five

I'm not sure if I'm living in the extremes, but I sure feel overwhelmed most of the time. How can I recognize when I'm being codependent?

Codependency happens when a current life event produces an inner response or an overreaction that is left over from the past. When this happens, you become re-traumatized. If you become involved in an abusive situation that echoes your past, if you trusted someone and they betrayed that trust or if your husband criticizes you in the same way your mother did and pulls away his love, you could end up feeling abandoned and be snapped back to your past. Whenever you are feeling out of control emotionally, it is a set-up for a codependent response. You may need to do Inner Child work.

Think about...

Think back to when you were a child, perhaps five years old. See yourself, your clothes, where you are, what you are doing. Recall any special sounds or smells of that time. Imagine how you must have felt, as that very young child.

Move your body into a position that best represents this mind-picture. Notice how you feel.

After a time write a short letter to yourself as that child, telling your child what you most needed to hear.

Question Thirty-Six

What is an Inner Child?

The *Inner Child* is a simple but profound concept that works in the healing process. The Inner Child embodies the emotions, images, memories and brain patterns that we experienced as a child and that we still retain as an adult. The Inner Child is a complex part of our emotional and survival system. It differs in nature and function from our intellect. It is a deep part of our human heritage born out of our Divine Nature. Soul has many dimensions. Our Soul includes but is not limited to the Inner Child. The Inner Child is the earliest, most primitive and deepest part of our Soul development.

The psychologist Carl Jung called it an Archetype. The Divine Child, along with Mother, Father and others, occurs in all cultures and through all time. The Child is natural, spontaneous and creative. The Child is a symbol of new life, energy and healing. When our Inner Child becomes whole through recovery, we can start over with a sense of wonder and newness about the world. It is as if we have been reborn to ourselves. We have retrieved our Inner Child Soul.

Think about...

Get an object that symbolizes your Inner Child and keep it near you. It can be a doll, a stuffed animal, a toy, a picture. Why does this object symbolize your Inner Child?

What feelings does it evoke in you?

Question Thirty-Seven

But I don't feel "divine" at all. I feel hurt and angry. Is there something wrong with me?

When we don't feel divine, it's because our Inner Child has been wounded. Each of us holds within ourselves many different Inner Children. They are like the ancient nested dolls from Russia that our children play with. There is a large, beautifully painted doll and when we turn her, she opens to reveal another, smaller doll, who in turn contains yet another, smaller doll and so on until we reach the smallest doll, the Divine Child. It is as if our energy has gotten trapped in pockets of feelings, images and memories that happened at different times.

If we examine our own inner world, we may find a happy two-year-old, an average four-year-old, but a seven-year-old who is suffering horrible and hurtful things in her life that happened "after we moved." The thirteen, sixteen or eighteen-year-old may be wounded in still other ways.

The pockets of energy are like ghosts of the past. All of these ghosts are trapped within our BodyMindSoul and they need to be freed during recovery.

We need to put ourselves in a safe and healing place when we open our dolls. Then we can soothe, relieve, ease and comfort all of our Inner Children. We can teach and strengthen all of them. We need to croon ancient lullabies to our Inner Children until we fall asleep with the peaceful tranquility and innocent trust that is our God-given birthright.

Think about...

Close your eyes and meditate upon the little children that you once were, noticing ages and places. When you open your eyes, draw what you experienced.

PROCESSES:

Question Thirty-Eight

I'm a professional in the field of chemical dependency. I recently gave a workshop to other professionals. I talked about shame and recognizing shame in ourselves before we can recognize it in our clients. I had them "experience shame" by drawing their own feelings of shame or about shame.

The response I got was ridicule, anger and judgment directed at me. It was a horrible experience for me and took weeks to get over. Can you explain what happened?

It is as if there is a deep mine field of shame inside of BodyMindSpirit and other people have detonators. The mine field was created by childhood blaming and shaming. It gets activated by other people through the mechanism of expectations when a similar situation or elements of that situation occur.

For example, if I am a participant and am expected to take something away from the workshop that I can use in my profession, then I cannot get too personally involved. I am expected to have it all together, especially in the helping professions. However, when my shame is activated by re-experiencing it, I do get personally involved.

In defense, I get into my cognitive and judgmental mode and begin to blame the workshop leader. I say things like, We're all professionals here. Isn't this rather elementary?" "This material is inappropriate for the level of intelligence in your audience." and "We really don't like experiential work at our school."

Through the process of blaming and judging, the shame in ourselves is reduced and transferred to another — that is, to the workshop leader or any other authority figure.

Now, let's look at the experience of the leader. She presents the shame material openly and she expects to be understood. When she feels the blame from the participants, she takes on their shame, just as she took on the shame of her parents as a child. She feels smaller. She remembers...

"If I was a better girl, Daddy wouldn't drink. Then Mommy wouldn't feel so bad. I wonder why I'm so bad..."

And even deeper, unconsciously...

Daddy feels bad about himself. He feels guilty and ashamed of himself for drinking. But he doesn't say this. He blames his boss, his wife, his stress, for his drinking. But the overly sensitive child, to whom nothing is ever communicated openly, receives *his* shame as *her own*. She is wide open at this tender age. Children at early ages gather information about the world through their senses. They see things like body language, drunken behavior, tears, looks in the eyes of parents. They *hear* the blaming and shaming statements (if it weren't for the children...if you gave me more attention...I wouldn't have to drink). They *feel* the tension...what will happen next? They have no labels for these sensations so they internalize the feelings as their own, much as they internalize the values, morals and customs of their environment. This happens over and over and soon the child develops deep inside of her, wells or pits, experienced as a lump in the stomach or a tightness in the heart. And the child learns that the way to transfer shame is to blame.

"I'm a bad person and I'm ashamed to be here, in the way. I'll hit my playmate or my doll so I'll feel better."

Sometimes this occurs through covert shaming. See the next question on covert shaming.

Think about...

Make a list of situations in which you felt shame. Notice what you focused on during your shame attack.

Question Thirty-Nine

What do you mean by covert shaming?

Covert shaming begins with all good motivations. An Adult Child is upset about his not doing well at a job. He turns to his mother for emotional support about this problem. Mother sees the son's pain and becomes defensive *for* him. She says things like, "they don't deserve a great person like you. You're too good to work for them anyway" and, as she warms to the subject, "What is a good person like you, a person with your intellectual ability and social skills, doing working at a low-level job like that? You're *better* than that!" This is a subtle put-down, clothed as a compliment.

The son begins with anger at the place of business that treated him badly. He is blaming. As Mother tries to "comfort" him, albeit well-intentioned, he begins to feel badly about himself. He agrees with her. Yes, it's a crumby place to work and he's better than that. Secretly, he feels ashamed of himself for being needy and caring about the opinions of others, and not being good enough.

Covertly, she is transferring her shame onto him. She feels ashamed of herself for having raised a son who does not live up to his potential. She sees how sad he feels...his head is bowed, his shoulders rounded, his face is pained. She feels *terrible* for him and *guilty* for herself. So she begins her "up" lecture: "When I was your age..." She thinks she's providing a model for him, but she is really shaming him, telling him he's not good enough, less than she. Unknowingly, she's competing with him. This is how shame is transferred covertly and subtly. The child within gets the old mothermessage.

The son goes away feeling inadequate and shamed, then he becomes very angry with Mother but doesn't know why. So he adds to himself more shame for being angry with Mother. She was only trying to help him. He should be glad he has someone to turn to...someone who will listen...(Since he can't ever trust himself)

How different this scenario might have been if Mother were tuned in to her own feelings. She might have just listened to her son instead of identifying with him to the point where he was a reflection of her and her needs...just as she did when he was a child.

How different this scene might have been if Son had been in recovery and had been able to tune in when he was feeling *her* shame. If he had been able to recognize her *blame*, and his own, he might have felt differently. He might have discussed it with her. She might have responded with truth.

How different that encounter might have been for both of them, in recovery. In truth. But shame siphons off our power and leaves us with nothing but a bowed head, rounded shoulders and a face filled with pain.

Think about...

Draw how shame feels.

Question Forty

I can't go to church any more. Since my husband's DUI (Driving Under the Influence) accident in which one person was killed, I am so ashamed I can't face anyone. I feel like I've lost contact with God, too. I just feel like God isn't there any more.

Going to church and loving God is multi-dimensional. One dimension is the *spiritual*. It is my relationship with God as I understand Him. My relationship with God is very personal, very subjective and between just the two of us. How I handle myself in that relationship is going to be my personal choice. Sometimes I get angry with God and then I tell Him about it. Sometimes I am grateful and I tell Him that, too. Sometimes God and I have a dialogue, but His voice is hard to hear. Only in the silence of deep meditation can I even begin to listen to the voice of my God.

Another dimension is *emotional*. These are my feelings about God, church, people, my problems. This level lives in my body. Sometimes I confuse God and my parents. My feelings are valid and real and I sometimes bring them to God. But sometimes I also bring my feelings to other people. I relate to others on an emotional basis. I feel emotions no matter what I do. I often think my emotions are a barometer and show me the difference between my relationship with my God and my relationships with other people.

The last dimension has to do with the *social organization* that makes up the church of my choice. These are the people, clergy and laity with whom I interact when I attend church or affairs sponsored by the church. My shame lies at this level. I may feel shame in front of the people there. I don't confuse my church with my God. So I can feel no shame in my relationship with God. God is too special, too vast and too awesome for that.

Think about...

Write a letter to God explaining how you feel.

Question Forty-One

Why do I always seek out negative people who put me down?

Childhood experiences create unconscious memory patterns deep within our BodyMindSoul. Let us imagine that our interior life is like the terrain of the earth. We have mountains, rivers, oceans, lakes, plains, deserts inside. We have been over the same ground many times in our childhood and adulthood.

But we now see that there are some markers here. There are even some signs on the mountains, oceans and deserts of our interior life. Each sign marks different feelings: shame, fear, anger, disappointment, guilt, sadness. As a child, each person, situation and event in our lives created a mound that lies under the marker for us. As children, we could not name or understand those feelings. But we have become *familiar* with the markers. We have often encountered them. We recognize them. We know them well.

Then we grow up. People, situations and events happen to us. We are *familiar* with only some of them. When we have that familiar feeling, we may even think we are *comfortable* with what is happening.

Familiarity and comfort are two different feelings. When we get in touch with how we feel, we can look beneath the familiar to see if we truly are *comfortable*. To comfort is to soothe, ease and relieve. With comfort, there is a sense of well-being. Familiarity holds no such feeling of well-being, only of knowledge.

For example, when someone gives a compliment or a nurturing remark, if we do not have a sign pointing to a familiar feeling to attach that to, we tend to let it go and it falls out of short-term memory. If, however, someone is critical and we internally recognize the signals of criticism or blame which lead to the familiar feelings of shame deep within us, then we say that our shame is activated. This is much like the pollen that triggers a sneeze in an allergic person. We are sensitized to certain things. We are not necessarily comfortable with them. We are usually unaware of this process and so it continues on and on, throughout adulthood.

93

To a person looking at our lives from the outside, it may seem as if we seek only negative, critical people to be around. To us, painful as it may be, these are the only signs with which we are familiar. Don't mistake familiarity for comfort.

Think about…

Who is the most negative person in your life?

Notice when you are most comfortable, using our definition.

Question Forty-Two

How do I change the unconscious memory patterns which make me seek out and accept negative people and experiences and reject positive people and experiences? I don't take compliments well.

The solution to this is to become aware of the patterns. Label signs and recognize and acknowledge feelings. If a fear trigger for me is a loved one raising his voice, then I need to stop right then and feel my fear when it happens. Accept rather than reject feelings of fear or anger.

Create an image for fear, like a purple color or a monster in black. Do not repeat any damaging words you hear. When we hear, see or experience something positive in our lives, such as a person telling us we look nice, we can try to picture what they are saying, like "me in a blue dress." Then, make ourselves look good in our image, even if at first we don't believe it. Repeat the compliment three times while taking deep breaths. Deep breaths help to relax and take in the feelings.

We usually repeat only the negatives such as, "and then he said, 'oh, why don't you shut up!'" rather than, "and then he said, 'you look nice in that dress.'"

Although we may feel that the good things do not penetrate our depths, have patience with the process. Learning takes practice. Remember when we learned to ride a bike or water ski? When we fell down, we got back up and tried again. Try to imagine that you swallow the good things. Eventually a new, small pool of feelings will be formed out of the positive input. We will begin to recognize the signs and signals of new feelings. When we begin to feel good about ourselves, we may hear our hearts sing softly. Listen for the sound.

Soon other people will hear your heart sing and come to listen, too.

Think about...

What did you tell yourself the last time you received a compliment?

Question Forty-Three

I never realized how much my past has affected my present life. Will I ever get well?

Yes, recovery works! When we realize how deeply wounded we've been, there is nothing to do but to walk through the wounds to the other side. Sometimes we need a hand to hold as we walk through the tunnel of pain and lance our own infections. Take your Inner Child by the hand and guide her through to freedom and peace. Feed and nourish your Inner Child because she was neglected, stabbed and mutilated. We can recognize when our Inner Child is starving when someone shows us tenderness or even when we hear about something nice one person has done for another and we choke up and want to cry.

We can feel our tight throat and broken heart. Inner loneliness is starvation. Our Inner Child desperately needs attention, comfort and encouragement to show herself to us.

We tend to treat ourselves as we were treated. When we begin to treat ourselves as we were not treated and begin to nurture and accept ourselves, the healing begins. There is hope.

Think about...

How can you nourish and feed your Inner Child?

Name some ways you can be more spontaneous.

How can you show more compassion toward that tender, young part of yourself?

Question Forty-Four

I feel like I live my life on a razor's edge of mood swings. I feel split apart. Am I schizophrenic?

In each of us there is a solid core of wholeness. We are born with a soul that has a capacity to experience the full spectrum of life. The innate ability of our soul expresses itself through imagination and it recreates the world anew every day. We have only to watch a very young child to know this.

Our wholeness is split with the axe of abuse. Our soul gets squashed, smashed and squeezed out when the basic split occurs. A hairline crack begins in the soul of a child the first time he is ignored rather than nurtured. The crack widens every single time his soul is deceived, misused or humiliated.

After a while, we have lost many parts of our original soul. We are no longer imaginative, creative or the author of our own lives. Now, rather than experiencing the fullness of life, we twist our lives in a caricature of living as we search out ever greater thrills or we numb our souls into oblivion.

And we don't know that we are mourning the loss of our soul-parts. And we wonder why creativity disappears into the holes in our adult lives.

Yes, we are fragmented. We are split in half. On one side we are the angry rebel or the seductive addict who is yearning for something he never had and craving excitement, while at the same time he is hiding, sneaking, lying and living on the knife's edge.

On the other side, we are the compliant codependent, the people-pleaser who is smiling, acting phony and wearing the false mask of codependency as he wonders what is wrong.

The more a person acts out his rebellious addict, the more shame he feels and the more he blames himself or others. Yet, when he acts on his people-pleasing half, he becomes more and more enraged, until there is a big blow-up and he uses again, gets sick, or kills someone.

You are not schizophrenic. You are codependent. Please seek out help. You do not have to be torn apart by your emotional swings. The conflicts can be resolved. *You* are more than your feelings. *You* are more than your moods. *You* are more than your conflicts. Allow your natural, spontaneous soul to emerge from the chaos and you'll be able to sit in the sun again as one whole, experiencing person without fear of going crazy. You will no longer over-react, out of the core of your fear. You will begin to react more moderately, out of the core of your own, original soul.

Think about…

How does your addict show up in your daily life?

How does your people-pleaser act today?

Question Forty-Five

What does it mean to overreact?

Since feelings are stored in the body, we may become flooded with feeling memories that are left over from past experiences. Even when our conscious mind does not remember events, our bodies have their own wisdom and they do remember. When these memories are touched, we are flooded with feelings.

For example, John does not call Alice on the day he said he would, but calls a day later. Alice goes into a panic and is sure that John doesn't love her any more. She is sure he has found someone better. When he does call, she is very angry and unreasonable and will not discuss it. She stores his behavior away in her inside pocket to be pulled out later.

Alice has overreacted. What Alice does not consciously remember is that when she was a child, her father would promise to take her to a ball game. She would get all ready to go. She'd wait...and wait...and wait. Her father would never come home. He would not even call. He'd forget. He'd be drunk.

Today, Alice reacts to John as if her father had forgotten his promise one more time. She becomes flooded with left over feelings from the past. Part of her soul disappears each time her father disappoints her and plays games with her trust.

Think about…

When was the last time you over-reacted?

How did you know you over-reacted?

How can you begin to act for yourself rather than over-react with left-over feelings from your past?

Question Forty-Six

OK, but what do I do with my strong feelings about things, especially when people don't call when they say they will? Wouldn't anyone be mad?

Some reaction is natural, but the codependent will act out these feelings and become "an angry person," exploding at the least provocation as if her insides held a time-bomb. She may build up her anger and binge on anger periodically with a rip-roaring temper tantrum that leaves her exhausted, empty and ashamed. Or the codependent may avoid any and all emotionally laden situations. He may get into work that is entirely logical and non-emotional. He can also numb out his feelings with a chemical substance, nicotine, food or with an activity such as shopping, spending, gambling or sexual activity.

When we act out our feelings in non-productive ways, the original emotions remain stored and seem to be impacted, as if they lie in a solid lump of radioactive toxic waste.

The rush of strong emotions such as you are experiencing can be extremely frightening. Naming and talking about the feelings defuses their power. Therapy is like a bomb squad, dismantling and rendering harmless the toxic substance.

Think about…

Do you feel a time-bomb inside of you?

How do you overreact?

When does this happen?

Question Forty-Seven

I've been told I suppress my emotions. Is that the same as repressing them?

No. In *repression*, we press our feelings back. Back into our body and away from our conscious awareness, they become impacted. Have you ever seen a fossil? The shape of an animal is imprinted into the earth's crust. In repression we become invisibly fossilized. We are not aware of the footprint of our history on our soul.

In *suppression*, we are aware of what we are feeling, but we choose not to express it. However, feelings that we hold inside, even though they are set off by current events, seem to stick to the fossilized core. There is a huge build-up and a consequent emotional charge to these feelings. We know we've touched a core issue when the suppressed feelings come to the surface and we over-react. This results in powerloss as we lose bits of our souls.

Repression can cause us to become sick. As long as we hide our emotions and don't express the way we feel, we will continue to get physically sick, often acting out our repressed emotions through our bodies. We will live a life full of codependent reactions. There are many correlations between a certain emotional orientation to life's problems and the types of illnesses people get. A person who represses anger, for example, may find himself having headaches of unknown origin.

Repression is more damaging than suppression but even when we suppress our honest feelings, we will live a life of codependent reactions. Codependency is like emphysema: chronic, debilitating and terminal. It is a process which has a traceable path and a trajectory with a predictable outcome.

Without treatment, we don't outgrow it and we don't gain wisdom and tranquility. We just get worse. Our hope is in commitment to recovery.

Think about...

What specific emotions do you think you carry in your body?

Where do you seem to carry them?

How could you learn to recognize and express more of your feelings?

Draw your body and your feelings in it.

Question Forty-Eight

How do I know if I am suppressing my feelings? Isn't there such a thing as healthy self-control?

The difference between healthy self-control and emotional suppression is *choice*. We have no choice when our usual response to certain situations or particular people is always the same. We are not free when we have one major feeling that comes up in response to almost everything. This feeling may be anger, fear or depression. Such a feeling is like a grayness that washes over all the colors in our lives, and it is always the same response.

When we are emotionally free, we keep our options open. We see the many choices that are available to us. We feel good about ourselves and take responsibility for our choices. To be emotionally healthy is to express free and appropriate feelings. Internal freedom is a free-flowing emotional energy. Free emotional energy is the greatest natural resource we have. A blocked emotional response is like locked doors and windows, rusted or painted shut and covered with spider webs in hidden rooms of our house. No matter how hard we try, we cannot go near those hidden rooms.

Free emotional response means that we are *willing* to search out and *are able* to open any or all doors and windows in our home *when we choose*. The sunshine and warm breezes flow through. Our home smells sweet and we are free and *alive*.

Think about...

When was the last time you exercised self-control?

What brought it up?

Think about an incident where you thought you were controlling yourself.

Might it have been suppression instead?

Question Forty-Nine

Why do I feel like I'm being punished whenever anything goes wrong in my life, especially anything emotional?

Remember that feelings in troubled families are not only de-emphasized but the *expression* of emotions is punished. If we get scared or become angry, we cannot express these feelings, we have to stuff them deep inside ourselves. Feelings that are pushed, stuffed or packed inside erupt in different ways.

You may be unconsciously angry but are afraid to express your anger, so you turn your anger inward. Punishing ourselves takes various forms: compulsive overeating or starving ourselves (anorexia), overspending or depriving ourselves by not allowing ourselves a vacation. You may have been a child of emotional deprivation.

Think about…

How do you punish yourself in your current life?

Over-eating?

Overspending?

Emotional hiding?

Question Fifty

What is emotional deprivation?

Emotional deprivation is best described by Jason, who tells us his story. "On the surface, our home seemed pretty good. There was no alcohol and no physical abuse. No one even criticized much. For a long time, I blamed myself for my depression. But in recovery, I saw that what I suffered from was real.

"No, there was no alcohol or physical abuse, but no one cared enough to yell. My dad was depressed. He never bent down to my level when I was a child. Everything revolved around what he wanted. *His* needs were always more important than ours. I think he was scared of his own kids. He was a kid himself. He was jealous of his boys.

"It's not too strong to say that I felt like I had no right to live, no right to any needs at all. I died a spiritual death as a child, through the emotional deprivation of any real caring or attention, negative or positive.

"It's taken me years to find my own power because it was taken away by severe emotional neglect."

Think about...

Does this story fit you?

Where does it fit and where does it not fit?

Question Fifty-One

Besides have trouble with emotional feelings, I also seem to be sick more than others. Can our emotions show up in illness? Feelings are one thing. My body is another. Please help me.

Emotions that are not acknowledged and expressed are stored in various tissues and organs of our body. We carry our feelings in our body. Repressed emotions are a sign of Codependency. Codependency can be a dangerous state and even in recovery, we can experience various bodily symptoms and sensations. We may have shooting pains in arms and legs, difficulty in breathing and swallowing, tightness in the chest that can be symptomatic of unexpressed feelings. Knots in our stomach, jaw and tooth problems, and even arthritic pains in deep muscle groups can be symptoms of codependency in hiding.

Many experts agree that ulcers, colitis, asthma, undefined headaches, heart disease and certain forms of cancer are often stress-induced or compounded by stress in our lives. The BodyMindSoul is a unit. What is not expressed is repressed. What is repressed is acted out in the body. If you have any of these conditions, please see a medical doctor but do not ignore the possibility that your body is signaling to you that something is wrong. One of the hopes of our times is that we do not have to get sick from our unacknowledged and unexpressed feelings, to finally get help.

Think about...

What body symptoms do you have that might be hidden codependency?

Rashes?

Colitis?

Headaches?

Back problems?

Draw your body and its aches, pains and sufferings.

Question Fifty-Two

Since I've become more assertive and am saying how I feel, that is, that I'm angry with my husband, I feel worse. My whole body is reacting. My migraine headaches are worse and my skin is breaking out. I can hardly breathe. What is happening?

What is happening is that the emotions long repressed are surfacing for you now. When you were a child and you felt an emotion, especially anger or fear, you may have been afraid to express it. You held that feeling inside of you.

Like other young animals, children are highly sensitive to signals from parents, especially danger signals. We depend on our parents for our basic survival. Because of this, if we pick up fear in a parent, we feel their fear as our very own. The world is unsafe.

Unlike other animals, we communicate with words. And the words are often meaningless or false. If our parents tell us that a visit to the dentist will not be painful, or if they say, "Don't be a baby." or "I'll give you something to cry about," the parent does not deal with the truth.

Then we doubt our own reality. We learn not to feel appropriate emotions. We are afraid to show how we feel. We smile when we want to cry.

Janie looked up at her mother's face. Something was wrong with Mama. Mama hurried her along, handling her roughly. Her mouth was a straight line. Mama would get this funny look on her face all the time. But when Janie asked, "What's wrong, Mama?" Mama just got that tight-rope mouth and said, "Just be quiet. Don't make me nervous!"

Janie's stomach felt awful but she swallowed hard and tried to help Mama. Her throat hurt. Janie kept quiet. Her mouth got tight. She would not remember the painful incident later, but the terrible feelings would remain.

Now that Janie is grown up and people call her Jane, she notices that every time there's a sudden or unexpected change in plans, she overreacts and becomes confused, panicked or nauseous. She feels ashamed of herself for her feelings, and confused by her reaction. She doesn't remember being six-years-old. This may be what you are now feeling. Talk it over with someone you can trust. Take back your power. Bring back your soul.

Think about...

Write about the last time you became confused, panicky or nauseous.

What happened?

Who was involved?

What did it remind you of?

Question Fifty-Three

I don't know if I really love any more, not my husband, not my children, not myself. As a result I feel more like a prostitute than a wife, which doesn't help my self-esteem. I don't want a divorce. It would set a bad example for my kids and I have seen what divorce does to other families. I don't know what to do. Please help.

There are two parts to this question. One is how to find a way out of an impossible situation. The other is to think about love in new ways.

When we have tried everything we know how to do and nothing has worked and then we keep trying again and again, we use up our resources and become depleted. We can't think of one more thing to try. And we feel emptied of the energy to try. We move in circles, as if we were in a garden maze, with no flowers, no colors and no markers to show the way out.

The only way out of the maze seems to be to accept one of the unacceptable solutions we see. We can only change the situation, change ourselves or get out. This is a double-bind. In recovery, there may be some middle ground we haven't seen yet. It may not be necessary to accept *either* a divorce *or* the situation as it is.

When we're in a maze, it helps to stop trying to get out for a moment. Sit down in the middle. Take a few deep breaths. We've been here a long time. This is not a crisis situation. There is a world *outside* the maze. We just can't see, hear, smell or touch it right now. Get some help to sort this out.

When we realize that we've been addictive rather than loving, we wonder what love really is. Love is a connectedness, a relatedness. If we are all connected, then what happens to one of us happens to each of us. And when we love, we feel that connection. Loving begins with connection to our own beings and our God-self. Love is a mutuality, a giving and a receiving of the Spirit which we feel inside. We must begin with our own healing.

Think about...

Write down all the pros and cons of staying in, leaving the situation, and then try to generate new options.

Staying	Leaving

New Options

Question Fifty-Four

Is there a relationship between codependency and panic attacks?

Yes, there is a relationship. Panic attacks are one symptom of codependency. Anxiety is a general term for fear. Fear has a target. We are afraid of *something*, something concrete and specific. Fear is a response to a threat of *actual* danger. We can act on that reality.

A panic attack is a physiological and emotional response to a *perceived* threat. Our body reacts as if we were in terrible danger: heart rate increases, sweating occurs, adrenaline and other chemicals race through our body, preparing us for fight or flight. If we can't do either, we freeze. This is a classic stress response.

In a codependent relationship, we push away the thing we want and need the most and become terrified of that very separation. This creates a double-bind situation which feels dangerous to the personality. In panic attacks, we feel as if we cannot breathe and we will get killed or die of fright.

If we could talk during an attack, we might say something like, "I don't want to die but I don't know how to live." Panic arises out of helplessness. It is the *learned helplessness* of the neglected or abused child.

Think about…

Draw your last panic attack.

What happened to your body?

What color is your panic attack?

Question Fifty-Five

What is learned helplessness?

If we have been in a toxic environment, we have been in danger. If we've had no options and there has been no one there to protect us and if fear has been our constant companion, we have learned something. If these things have happened in our childhood when our bodies, minds and souls were completely open and vulnerable to our environment, we have learned that we have no power. We have learned that we are helpless to change the situation or our responses. We have learned "helplessness" as a response to fear. And we think it is a normal reaction.

Our Inner Child has incorporated feelings of helplessness, powerlessness and rage. Since he thinks he is his feelings, he becomes ineffective. He feels useless. Some people call this state depression. It is *really* soulloss. Our Inner Child has learned to sit in a corner, silently crying, "*Now* maybe they will see and hear me! I will stay here until someone comes to rescue me and take me out of this living hell. I have no power to change anything at all." *But no one comes*!

We have *learned* helplessness as a primary response to our world. We can learn new ways of being in the world. We can learn to replace powerlessness with empowerment. We can learn to retrieve our soul.

Think about…

How did you learn helplessness early in life?

What are some specific ways you can empower yourself now?

Question Fifty-Six

Can you explain passive-aggressive?

Passive-aggressive behavior is anger acted out in indirect ways. Sarcasm, non-verbal stubbornness and indirect verbal communication through another person are forms of passive-aggressive behavior. This behavior comes from being victimized and shamed in childhood. Because we feel powerless as adults, we give other people the power to run our lives. But then we resent them for it!

Passive-aggressive behavior is a child's way of getting even with the unfairness he finds around him. It arises out of lack of clarity and openness and fear of confrontation. It is an unwillingness to take responsibility for changing a situation because we've never been able to feel effective in our lives.

Work-related examples include an employee who resents her job and consistently comes in late or leaves early, a person who sits in a committee meeting with arms folded and won't participate because she feels forced to attend and a boss who won't discuss specific performance but who gives a low evaluation to his employee without warning.

Examples that happen in a family are a sister who forgets to give phone messages to her more popular sibling, a brother who spills a soft drink on the homework of brother John who "always gets good grades, only because he's such a nerd!" and a husband who procrastinates on a home repair project because "she's never satisfied anyway," but who won't say he doesn't want to do it.

Unspoken messages may be:

If I tell my boss how I feel, he'll probably fire me. I'm not good enough to get another job.

I may be forced to be here, but I'll let them know I'm not happy. Maybe then they'll pay attention.

I'm not happy with my employee, but I don't want to be accountable for explaining why. I might be wrong and then I'd look bad.

I'll never be as good as him. He gets it all and I get nothing.

If I say no, he will leave me.

If she knows how I am, she won't love me.

Passive-aggressive behavior is hiding behavior. It is a cover-up for low self-esteem, inadequacies and fear. At bottom, passive-aggressive is a hallmark of a shame-based person who blames others to cover his own shame.

At even deeper levels, this behavior hides terror of abandonment. The internal talk runs, "I'm no good, a worthless piece of nothing and no one would want me anyway. It doesn't matter much what I do. Sooner or later, everyone will leave me."

And the passive-aggressive person continually sets himself up to prove himself right. Sooner or later, other people get tired of the hidden anger or the poor-me game and do leave. Powerloss causes desperation, despondency and the dis-spiritedness of a lost soul.

Think about...

Who are you most angry with?

How do you show your anger?

Passive?

Aggressive?

Passive-Aggressive?

How could you be more assertive?

124

Question Fifty-Seven

My friend says I project my anger onto her. I don't know what she means by this. Can you tell me what's wrong with her?

Projection is related to shame/blame. It is a defense mechanism which helps us deal with our overwhelming emotions by externalizing them. To project means to thrust or to hurl out. Emotionally, we attribute to other people emotions that we ourselves are feeling. We see in others what is inside of us. We take the emotional energy invested in a feeling and act as if it belongs to another person rather than ourselves. We act as if someone else caused our pain.

To overcome this defense, we can use the Mirror Concept, which will be discussed in the next question.

Think about...

When was the last time you projected your feelings onto someone else?

On whom?

How did you do this?

How did the other person react?

Question Fifty-Eight

What is the mirror concept?

This is seeing ourselves in the attitudes, behavior and feelings of other people. We are related to others through feelings and we can see ourselves reflected in the behavior of others. For example, Carol notices that her friend blushes whenever they talk about something personal. She feels embarrassed for her friend and wants to help her. But of all the behaviors that her friend does, why is it that Carol notices only this particular one? Could it be that it is something inside of Carol herself? Blushing is related to embarrassment and that is shame. Possibly Carol has shame lurking inside of her.

It may help to notice when we see something in someone else and to ask, is this something I feel in myself? Am I expressing this quality in my own life? Is it something that I cannot express? What am I afraid to see in myself?

We unconsciously use other people to reflect back to us our own behavior but in the final analysis, we must own our own feelings, thoughts and behavior. When we own something, we take responsibility for it and then we can change it.

Think about...

Who in your life is your most helpful mirror right now?

Do you think there is truth in the saying: "That which we dislike most in others is something we have in ourselves"?

Can you find examples of this in your own experience?

PART THREE

Addictions

Social and Personal Addictions

Relationship Addictions

Helping Addictions

THE ADDICTIVE CYCLE

We've been discussing some ways in which we lose our power and our energy through trauma and abuse. Without power, we cannot initiate change or direct our lives in any meaningful way. Our deepest essence, the center of our BodyMind, becomes obscured. We disconnect from our own soul, the balance-beam of our very lives. We are blown about by outer forces. The winds howl through the holes inside of us. We have no ballast and we tumble about, mindlessly trying to find a stable position in a world that is overwhelming. The disconnection is complete.

We flail around, searching for a solution. We desperately need a calming center and a focus. We need power and energy. How shall we be saved? Ah!! We find an addiction! We immediately feel a sense of comfort — freedom, for a time, from the emptiness. Relief from the pain. We feel a false sense of power when we use our addiction. Our perception of helplessness changes and we fool ourselves for a time.

Inside we feel empty, isolated and forlorn. We hide from ourselves and present a false mask to the world. All the while, we know that our lives are out of balance. We begin the addictive cycle.

Question Fifty-Nine

What is the addictive cycle?

A person begins the addictive cycle with FAPS: Fear, Anger, Pain, Shame. He feels helpless and out of control. He wants to avoid feeling this way. He knows what will help him. His old addiction, whatever it is.

He begins to think about and to plan to use his addiction. At first, it works very well. He feels some control and lots of excitement or tranquility (depending on which form he uses). He has great hope that this time the outcome will be different.

He moves up the cycle wall a little at a time until he reaches the pinnacle — the high — or the low — and Boom! It's too late! The addiction takes over and he loses control, excitement and hope.

Intervention, either formal or personal must take place before the person reaches the top of the cycle.

THE ADDICTIVE CYCLE

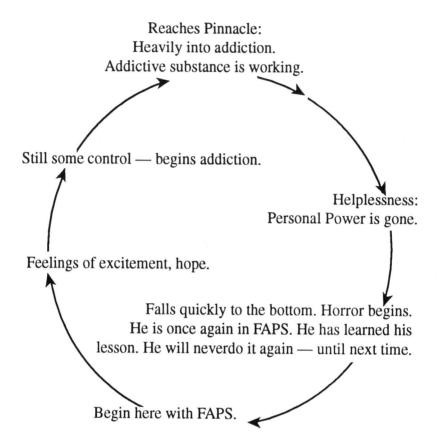

Reaches Pinnacle:
Heavily into addiction.
Addictive substance is working.

Still some control — begins addiction.

Helplessness:
Personal Power is gone.

Feelings of excitement, hope.

Falls quickly to the bottom. Horror begins.
He is once again in FAPS. He has learned his
lesson. He will neverdo it again — until next time.

Begin here with FAPS.

Question Sixty

I can see being an alcoholic or drug addict. But can someone really be addicted to normal activities like running, TV or...can I really be a workaholic?

It is not the use of alcohol which creates alcoholism. It is the abuse of alcohol. We focus on alcohol to avoid our relationships. Likewise, it is not the use of work or valuing work which creates workaholism. When we use work and work-related activities to avoid intimacy and closeness with others, especially family members, we need to look to our true motivation.

There are activities which produce in themselves and of themselves certain emotional states in ourselves. Running and certain forms of other exercise create BodyMindSoul states that are different from a neutral or resting state. We become habituated to various body states, often without our conscious knowledge. The accommodation to the "high" of work occurs on a cellular level, as does alcohol addiction. Then we suspect workaholism.

Think about...

How do you emotionally use your work?

How do you feel when you have unstructured time, say, on the weekends?

Question Sixty-One

Is there a relationship between codependency and physical fitness?

Yes. People who are codependent live on the edges. We have extreme feelings about our bodies. One extreme is that we compulsively work out to the point of exhaustion, magnify flaws like gray hair, fat calves and double chins in our urgency to be perfect, and we can become too thin.

The other extreme is that we don't pay attention to health, cholesterol levels and proper nutrition. We have the exaggerated idea that we don't deserve to feel good, look good or to be healthy, and we may become a compulsive overeater.

Exaggerated behavior can signal an addiction. Addictive behavior happens too much, too fast and we become hooked on the quick fix. A physically fit person can also be addicted, however. Look to the motivation.

Think about...

What are your exaggerated behaviors?

How do you feel when you do these behaviors?

How do you feel when you don't?

Have you ever tried to change one of these behaviors?

What happened?

Question Sixty-Two

I am a recovering alcoholic and have not touched alcohol for ten years. My wife, a recovering codependent, tells me that my reading habits are causing us problems. She says I never have time for her. I like to read and listen to music. What's so wrong about that?

We use our addictions as a primary way of *regulating* our behavior. They work to keep a balance in our systems. We also use addictions to *avoid* dealing with our inner lives and our relationships. We use them to *fill* ourselves up.

There are basically two forms of addictions, whether they are chemically, physically or emotionally induced. In the *arousal* state, we look for potency, energy and excitement. At the other end are *satiation* addictions in which we look for permanence, predictability and satisfaction.

There are certain activities in our culture which are socially acceptable, even socially desirable, which produce states of euphoria, heightened sensibilities, high sensitivities, adrenaline rushes and so forth. Some of these activities are work, sex, shopping and exercise.

Other activities stimulate chemicals which interact in our bodies to produce a steady, quiet state. They even out our moods, calm us down and give us serenity. Some of these activities are meditation, reading, watching TV and eating certain kinds of foods in ritualistic ways. You may have noticed that your Alcoholics Anonymous meetings do this for you, spiritually.

None of these activities in itself is harmful. All are helpful and necessary. The point is that it is not a particular activity which can be addictive, but it is the way the activity is used and sometimes abused, that creates a problem. When one addiction gets us into trouble, we often switch to another. In this way, we avoid dealing with the underlying problems. We go around and around the addictive cycle. And we keep up the self-deception.

We may have several addictions going at once. We switch from one to another of our arousal addictions (Group A) to get the high excitement our MindBody needs at a particular time

or

we may switch from one to another of our satiation addictions (Group B) to get the relief and comfort we need at another point in time.

or

we switch addictions, from Group A to B and vice versa. In this way, we regulate our behavior and fool ourselves into thinking/feeling that we are well and in control of our lives. The process looks like this:

SWITCHING ADDICTIONS

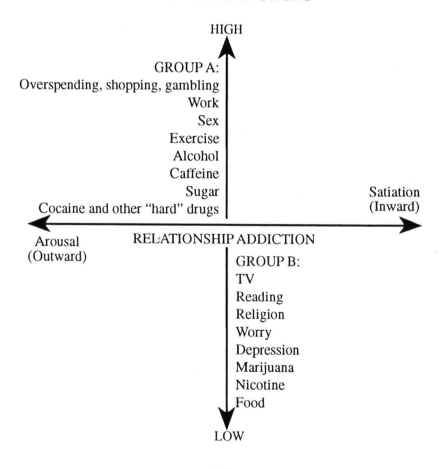

All of the above activities are normal, necessary and satisfying, if we use them to balance and enrich our lives. Some begin with a high and end with a low, especially addictive relationships. Some offer soothing relief from inner anxieties and tensions. Others are comforting and restful. Still others seem to be a source of strength for us. We need only to be aware of our motivations and our excesses to stay centered and in balance.

Balancing our lives with addictive activities looks like this:

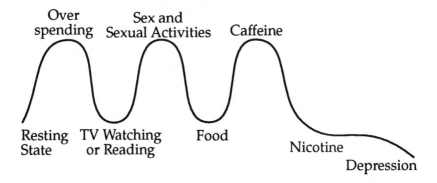

We may or may not have an addictive relationship going on at the same time.

If we use our activities as a means of avoiding responsibility for our intimate relationships or if we allow ourselves to become im-balanced through abuse of these normal activities, then we can say we are addicted.

Question Sixty-Three

I find myself gaining more and more weight. Sometimes I eat when I'm not hungry. What is wrong with me?

Eating disorders are a part of codependency. If we were not taken care of as children, we do not learn to care for ourselves. We compulsively overeat to relieve the pain of a childhood when we were neglected or abandoned. When we overeat, our stomachs stretch and soon we do not recognize whether we are physically hungry or emotionally hungry.

At the other extreme, under-eating can be a form of self-punishment. It is natural to like food and cooking can be a creative art. When we stuff or deprive our bodies, it is not natural but often it is a result of experiencing a "hole inside" that is never filled. It is the hole of a deprived soul.

Think about...

What are your favorite foods?

How do you use food?

As comfort?

When you eat, do you feel drugged?

Do you use food to numb-out?

As anger release?

To avoid what?

Question Sixty-Four

I think I know what you mean, but I'm not sure. Tell me more about the hole inside.

We all grow up with holes inside. It is the empty feeling in the pit of our stomach. It is stomach aches, poor digestion. It is ulcers. It is colitis. It is the hole of a lost soul.

Codependents look to something *outside* themselves and their own lost experience to fill that hole. But the hole can be, and needs to be, filled with you.

Try this image: Fill the hole with rich, black soil. Plant the seed called by your name. Give it the sunshine of self-love, the water of God's love and relentlessly pull every weed of self doubt out by the roots.

It will begin as a tiny green shoot. It will grow in its own way, at its own pace. You cannot hurry it. Do not dig it up to see if it is growing "right."

Inside your seed is the work of God, God's gift to the world. The work of recovery, of planting and tending the seed, of loving, honoring and cherishing it, is *yours*. It will be your gift to the world. Cherish the seed called by your name and nurture it to maturation.

Think about...

How did you feel when you did this exercise?

Draw your seed.

What specific things could you do to nurture your seed?

Question Sixty-Five

Does codependency affect your thinking? I seem to become confused easily these days.

Yes, codependency affects our thinking. A process that we may recognize when codependency is activated is that our heads feel stuffed. Thoughts and worries seem to lie right next to each other in rows like corn on the cob. Thoughts and worries are interlocked into each other and a tightness results when we try to figure something out. Our heads are filled with gears or a giant interlocking puzzle that we can't solve. Things won't fit together. If one worry drops out, we reach out and have to find another to take its place. We need our heads to be entirely filled.

If our heads are not filled with interlocking gears, we may feel as if we are mentally in a circular room. We have a thought or feeling or an impression and we run with it to the other side of the room, like the proverbial drunken monkey. There we bounce off the wall and we're in another place in the same room. Then we have another thought or feeling and we run with it to the other side of the room, where we bounce off that wall and we're in another place in the *same room*. Then we have another thought or feeling and we run with it...until we suddenly realize that we're always in the *same room*! This is called spinning thinking.

Think about...

What are you spinning about right now?

If you weren't spinning, what would you be doing?

...Feeling?

Question Sixty-Six

What is spinning thinking?

Spinning thinking is an obsessive thought pattern in which a person vacillates between parameters, veering from one thought to another.

It is a thought pattern in which irrelevancies and low priority thoughts are mixed in with important ideas and solutions. Everything is important while nothing is important. It is circular thinking with no priorities:

> I wonder what Joe is doing now that we're not together...I'll always be alone...I'm using caffeine again...he's probably found someone better...I've gotta lose some weight...I should go to the health club...there are pretty girls at the health club... I'm not pretty...I'm too fat...maybe I should call Joe...I should join Weight Watchers...I think I will call Joe...no, I'll wait til I lose some weight and then he'll be sorry...I won't even talk to him...maybe that's why Dad cheated on Mom...she wasn't that heavy...I didn't think she was...I wonder what Joe is doing now that we're not together...I'll always be alone...I'm going to give up caffeine right now...I'm going to get a hot fudge sundae right now...

It spirals into all of the parameters of a problem simultaneously rather than in any logical or prioritized order. It precludes any problem solving. It is a panic reaction. There are no boundaries in these thoughts. It's like living in the middle of a whirlpool, being sucked down and thrown around. No control. Out of control...spinning...spinning... spinning...spinning...

The purpose of spinning thinking is the same as that of all addictions. It keeps us from feeling anything. It keeps us from acting in any way to solve a problem. We use it to plug up our feelings and give the illusion of problem solving. It's a way of enabling ourselves not to feel, think, act or recover.

Think about...

When you begin to feel overwhelmed by a problem, pick up a pen and pad and sit down. Write without lifting the pen from the paper for ten minutes. When you have finished, notice the ways in which you avoided your feelings by jumping from one thing to another or going over the same thing again and again.

(P.S. One way to change this behavior is to state the primary problem in one sentence and then write a paragraph on how you feel about the issue.)

Question Sixty-Seven

One measure of success is not whether you have a problem, but whether it's the same problem you had last year. I seem to worry about the same things all the time. Can you talk about worries?

Worry can be divided into two classes, destructive and constructive. As codependents, we tend to worry a great deal. We seem to fill our minds with worry, until there's little room for anything else. Worry can be an addiction but it is also part of faulty problem solving.

Destructive worry is obsessive. We go over the elements of the problem. We go over the elements of the problem. Over and over and over. We won't accept any solution we come up with. We fill our minds with the problem and our hearts are heavy with it. We wake up at night worrying about it and worrying about it and worrying about it, like a dog with a bone.

This means that there is something that we have not let go of. Maybe we have not let go of our pride, not wanting to make a change. Possibly we're too proud to accept something that we need to accept. Or maybe we're too arrogant, thinking we can do it all alone, or that we're some kind of god. We may think it's totally up to us to make things happen the way we want them to happen. As codependents, we often feel a need to control outcomes ourselves. Or we think, superstitiously, that if we only worry *enough*, nothing bad will happen.

Neurotic worry occurs over a condition that does not seem necessary at all. Neurotic worry spills over into every area of life. It feels to the worrier that the whole problem could be avoided if the other person would only...just...and we *have* to worry. But do we?

Destructive or neurotic worry is often prefaced by certain key phrases, such as "If only..." and "It's not within my power to..."

Other phrases indicate hidden anger with the situation. Some of these phrases are:

"I can't understand why he..." "How could she..." and "I can't ..." or "I won't..."

When we hear ourselves subvocally using these phrases, it is time to surrender.

Constructive worry, on the other hand, looks like this: we go over the elements of a problem and at first, we see only two solutions, yes or no. But there may be other choices that we haven't looked at. In this case, we need to treat the matter as a problem to be solved rather than as a tragedy to be endured. Maybe we just need to feel angry, sad or bad. Maybe we just have to live with the problem or we might have to leave the situation. We might have to seek outside help.

A question to ask ourselves might be, what am I avoiding in myself by focusing on the problem of this other person? Whether we worry destructively, neurotically or constructively is a choice we make each and every day. It's a part of our recovery and healing to make good choices. It's up to us to recognize our own core issues and heal them.

Think about...

What is your major worry at this point in your life?

What was your major worry three months ago?

Six months ago?

How can you let go more and worry less?

Question Sixty-Eight

I seem to be addicted to hiring people to work for me that treat me as abusively as my mother. I know that I finally reach my limits with each of them and eventually fire them, but I need to know how to stop this cycle. It is draining me.

You may be addicted to abuse. Yes, reliving old hurts is draining. Knowing the signals of a potentially emotionally abusive relationship or person is very important. Deal with yourself gently. Don't beat yourself up for repeating the pattern you learned so well. The child within you is still looking for mother's love and still mistakes abuse for positive attention. Learn to set limits early in a relationship. I refer you to the question on Boundaries. Define the job limits and become aware of which behaviors, verbal or nonverbal, cross the boundary line.

The bottom line is, fire your mother. That is not meant to be either a silly statement or a hurtful one. If a parent is emotionally abusive, we have a right to fire her, divorce her, leave her emotionally and physically if need be. We have a right to live in the world free of abuse and able to take support from constructive others.

Think about...

Write a good-bye letter to your mother. Do not mail it.

Question Sixty-Nine

I know I'm a compulsive person. I spend so much that I keep myself impoverished in money and in spirit. There have been times when I walk into my closet and surround myself with my clothes. I even wrap my emotionally starved body in my clothes and try to feel good about myself. But it doesn't work. What is wrong with me?

You may be a spendaholic. A spending-addicted person will, if they *have* some money, just have to spend it. Then we have to *juggle* our bills around and *always* have to worry about not having enough money, even though there is adequate income. Remember that money, like sex, is a symbol of power. We translate love-and-attention-lack in childhood to money-lack in adulthood. Only now *we* make sure there is never enough to go around. This addiction can be treated just as other addictions. Do Inner Child work and give yourself the love and attention you missed. It will take time but it will work.

Think about…

Are your finances in control?

Does spending money make you feel good?

After you have over-spent, do you worry?

Do you feel guilty?

Question Seventy

Why am I such a perfectionist? It causes me so much trouble, but I can't seem to accept anything if it's less than perfect.

Perfectionism is really another addiction. It effectively keeps us out of our feelings and gives us something to focus on other than the source of our problem.

Perfectionism is a clear example of the If-Then Syndrome, living in the extremes. We say in effect, "If I am not perfect, then I am a failure." "If I don't get an A, then I get an F."

This comes as a result of living in the alcoholic or dysfunctional home and trying desperately to make father or mother stop drinking or be happy and consistently failing at the task. The results are instant. If mother or father still drinks, then we have clearly failed.

Perfectionism is also the result of fear of making a mistake. If everything we do has to be perfect, that means we cannot experiment. We cannot try. We cannot explore and we do not learn. And if we don't try, we cannot fail.

Perfectionism is also a cop-out. "If you can't do it right, don't do it at all." This is the result of a right-or-wrong mentality in an unhealthy home. There is no middle ground. There has to be a winner and a loser. So we continue to procrastinate because we won't be able to perfect the task, so we never start. Or we make everyone's life miserable trying to do it perfectly. And we have no tolerance for the mistakes of others either.

To strive for perfection is to kill love because perfection does not recognize the imperfect nature of humanity. It does not recognize our essence. It does not see our soul. It does not recognize balance. We are more than our perfectionism.

Think about...

What has your need to be best, to stand out, prevented you from doing?

How has it limited you in other ways?

How does your perfectionism show up in your personal relationships?

Question Seventy-One

My mother's reaction to my alcoholic father was to become very depressed. Most days she didn't even raise the blinds in the house but kept it always dark. Dark and cold. That's how I remember my childhood. It seems to me that my mother was sicker than my father. Don't you think she could have coped better?

That is hard to answer because we don't know all that your mother had to deal with. Your mother could have been codependent. Depression is often a symptom of codependency. The physical, sexual, emotional abuse in the backgrounds of many people, especially women, have not been taken seriously.

At one time in history, we have chained what were cruelly called "lunatics" to bedposts or have kept them in attic rooms. Until very recent years, psychologists and psychiatrists would routinely medicate and regularly hospitalize "victims" of clinical depression, anxiety and other mood disorders, missing the primary disease of codependency.

Depression is both biochemical and learned. This does not mean that medication should *never* be used to treat depression nor that medication should *always* be used, but only that each case must be evaluated carefully and all factors taken into account. Some people respond to both medication and psychotherapy. Also, symptoms may vary and people sometimes need to be in a hospital.

Each individual must be evaluated carefully by a professional who has background training and experience in addictions and codependency as well as traditional frameworks. We need to monitor all medications carefully, especially for any addictive potential.

Depression results from helplessness and hopelessness, from remaining a victim of circumstances in our lives. When we have been a victim for a very long time and nothing has changed, we become addicted to our depression. We have learned to cope by becoming depressed. We unconsciously find ways to feed our depression.

If we remember that we have choices about what happens to us and how we react to what happens to us, we come out of the darkness of depression and despair, into the sunlight of choice and freedom.

Think about...

How do you keep yourself a victim?

What is your darkened room like?

RELATIONSHIP ADDICTIONS

Question Seventy-Two

I love my boyfriend a lot and I do a lot to make him happy. But a big part of me feels numb and I have no energy most of the time. Can you explain what is happening?

Emotions or feelings are natural responses in our bodies to pleasure, pain or danger. If we have been hurt, it is natural to feel angry and to want to act on that feeling, perhaps to strike back.

Feelings in troubled families are de-emphasized and any expression of emotions is punished. So if, as children we feel upset by the conditions in our homes as children and distressed by the reactions in our body, we choose one of three responses:

- We can express our anger and take the risk of being annihilated.
- We can run away.
- We can numb out, freeze our feelings.

In an unhealthy home, expressing feelings, especially anger, is too dangerous. Running away is impossible for a child. So what is left? Not to feel anything, good or bad.

Emotions are chemicals manufactured and distributed in the body. If they are not expressed and thus released, they are stored deep in the cells and tissues of the body and deep in the guts of the child.

We need to have free access to the feelings because our motivation lies in our emotional responses. Emotions provide the passion that serves our best interests. If we have learned as children not to feel feelings but to numb ourselves out, we are essentially soul-dead. Motivation and passion are the natural result of freeing up our emotional energy.

In a relationship, emotional energy is a pouring out of ourselves into another person. When we give our emotional energy, we shower another person with our worry, our thoughts, our effort and our love, regardless of our own needs. In the beginning of a love relationship, this works fine. At first, we get as much as we give. We get the wonderful, high feeling of "falling in love". We get limerance, the feeling of being caught up and swept away. That's as it should be. But after the first blush has worn off, something changes.

In a longer-term relationship which by nature must be mutual, such as a marriage, love partnership or friendship, we naturally expect the other person to invest her emotional energy into us when we need it. We naturally expect to be thought about, cared about and occasionally worried about. That is mutuality. That is reciprocity.

If, on the other hand, we are in a relationship with a person who is not able or willing to give to us and care about our best interests as we do his, sooner or later, we will become dissatisfied. Anyone who continues to give without taking a turn and who empties himself without filling, is going to build up anger, resentments and bitterness. Mother Theresa is the epitome of giving without getting, but she fills herself up with her God.

We can learn to set reasonable limits and reasonable expectations on ourselves and others. Detachment does not mean not to love. There is more on detachment in another question. For our discussion, detachment means not giving what you can't give and not doing what you can't do. It means retrieving your soul.

Think about...

What was your primary reaction as a child to the impossible situation in which you found yourself?

Part of the Twelve-Step Program for codependents tells us that we must admit that we are powerless over our emotions and as a result, our lives have become unmanageable. Write a paragraph on how you are powerless over your emotions in your current relationship and list ten ways your life has become unmanageable as a result.

Question Seventy-Three

I get depressed when my boyfriend is mean to me. But he has a heart of gold. I just know how he is underneath, so I stay with him even though he hurts me a lot. How can I get him to show his good side more often?

Everyone has flaws. No one is perfect, but you may be addicted to potential. You may be in love with the person he could be rather than the person he is. Sounds like you could be playing the slot machine game: just one more try and I'll win the pot. When we do this, we live in the future rather than in the present. The future looks rosy, while the present is full of anxiety.

Now is the time to be deeply honest with yourself. When I was younger, I knew a man with "great potential". Everyone said he could be anything he wanted to be. It is now 20 years later and he has not changed at all. He has not realized his youthful potential.

Potential energy is not real energy. If you want to know how a person really is, watch his behavior.

Think about...

Draw your potential.

Question Seventy-Four

Do you think the solution to codependency is to get rid of the person causing the codependency?

No. That's blame, not responsibility. Another person does not "cause" codependency, but the interaction between two people creates a vulnerability that brings up codependent feelings.

Blame creates shame ... shame creates guilt ... guilt creates anger ... anger creates shame ... and we blame to get rid of the shame ... and we are caught in the cycle of blame/shame.

BLAME/SHAME CYCLE

In the beginning, Person A feels small, worthless, shame-full. With every hit to Person B, his ego grows to cover his shame and he feels bigger.

Conversely, with every hit taken by Person B, that person's ego shrinks until he reaches his own core-shame base, with which he is quite familiar.

Then the roles are reversed, either through aggressive action or through passive-aggressive inaction.

PERSON A (BLAMER)	PERSON B (BLAMED/SHAMED)
First Hit: Don't you ever notice what needs to be done around here? o — *Feels small*	Looks downcast Feels okay O — *Appears big*
Second Hit: Well, I can't do everything. You could at least take out the garbage for me. o — *Feels better*	I forgot. Feels less than okay O — *Appears smaller*

Third Hit:
Yeah, you forgot!   I know
What would happen if   Feels more inadequate
I forgot all the time?   o — *Appears smaller yet*
You know how hard I
work all day!
O — *Feels bigger*

Fourth Hit:
You oughtta be!   OK. I'm sorry
Whyn't ya do it right   o — *Looks and feels tiny*
now, since you can't   *and ashamed*
remember anything for
more than five minutes.
O — *Feels biggest*

This tirade can go on and on and on, taking as long as is necessary for Person A to feel better and for Person B to feel shamed.

By "hit" I mean any put-down, criticism, blaming or shaming remark, tirade, lecture or abuse.

By the end of the transaction, Person A has successfully transferred his shame onto Person B, who has successfully received the shame with which he feels completely familiar.

The interaction has been between two false, codependent egos rather than between two real and healthy persons.

A person learns to blame and shame because as a child he was blamed and shamed. Let us suppose that Bob is the person in power. He can be father, mother, husband, wife, lover, child or sibling. He begins with his left-over feelings of shame from childhood. He is already at the bottom of this cycle. As soon as he feels his shame, he transfers it to the only person available to him, his significant other. This is the person with whom he feels most vulnerable. In his system, vulnerability equals shame. He transfers it like this:

Bob, in his shame, is feeling very small and insignificant. He looks around for some reason, something to pin it on. He sees that the garbage hasn't been taken out, the car is dirty, he can't find his shoes, anything at all will do. When he finds the outer cause, he begins to berate, belittle and ridicule JoAnn. JoAnn's part in this is that she has given Bob her power, the power to invade her emotionally. So she will "take his shame", little by little.

With each verbal or physical attack, each hit or punch or pinch, he transfers more and more shame onto her. As a result, his ego becomes more and more inflated and she feels smaller and smaller, until she feels no power at all. This continues until his rage taps into her deepest fears, that she is really worthless and deserves to be unwanted, unloved and left to die!

When this happens, a codependent will react by either leaving abruptly or staying and becoming increasingly fearful and angry. Feeling helpless and powerless are signs of codependency. A healthy person will look at options for changing his own behavior. If this doesn't work and he is still unhappy, then he will leave. But not before checking out all options.

To break the cycle requires a shift from shame to love. Each person must take loving responsibility for only his or her own shame rather than that of the other. Not an easy job, but it can be done.

One of the ways that we recall our own soul is by breaking this vicious cycle.

Think about...

How do you get into the blame-shame cycle?

Does it help?

Question Seventy-Five

I am not attracted to alcoholics. So why do my friends think I'm codependent in my relationships with men?

Codependency takes many forms. We may not be attracted to men who abuse alcohol. But we may choose men who have other kinds of habits that can become addictive and keep them from being emotionally available to us. It interferes with the kind of closeness we want from another in an intimate relationship. We don't get what we need. The addiction may be to power or success or golf. It's probably there somewhere.

Are the men we choose in any way similar to one another? Do they work long hours and become very tired, too tired to go out a reasonable amount of time? Are they too tired or distracted to talk or do they talk only about their work and their day? Or do they hide behind a newspaper, a TV program, sporting events or a book so that interaction is often preceded by, "Ssh, this is an important part." or "Can't you see I'm watching this?"

His addictions may be hidden. Gambling addiction is often hidden behind playing the stock market, options or commodities excessively. The key is excess. One can become a trader with money that is needed for other things rather than with discretionary money.

Spending addiction is often masked by generosity or a high life style. We may love this part of him, until we see how he juggles and manipulates the bills when come due or overdue. Or how he hides extra money for his own pleasure. Depression may also be an addiction. And you may be counter-addicted to cheering him up. Examine how you give your power away to men.

Think about...

Are you concerned about any hidden addictions in yourself?

How so?

What are your clues?

Question Seventy-Six

It seems like my husband and I will never be happy. When one of us is successful, the other is not happy for them. It seems that we both can't be happy at the same time. We can't feel good for the other person, ever. What can we do?

What may be happening is that the two of you are doing a dance of competition rather than a dance of intimacy. When Adult Children marry, we often don't realize that marriage is a partnership which calls for teamwork. What benefits one will also benefit the other, because the two of you have a common life. We react to each other as we did to our siblings in our unhealthy home. You need to check this out with an objective third party.

Think about...

Is there a scarcity of good feelings for either or both of you?

How does this play itself out in your relationship?

Question Seventy-Seven

My father, who was an alcoholic, was a very domineering, manipulative person. My husband, who is not alcoholic, has the same behavior and personality. Did I choose him because of my own codependency?

Probably so. Familiarity beckons and we want what we can't get. The drinking behavior is not what attracts us. What we are attracted to is the personality or the "good parts". The unavailability of the person is glossed over in our need. When a relationship feels very familiar to us, we need to check out our own self-talk. "Oh, yeah, I know this one," we may say. Then we add, "but this time, it will be different." And it never is.

Once you have recognized and identified the similarities between your husband and your father, you must recognize and admit your own patterns of response. Begin by comparing and contrasting the two relationships, on the emotional level. You may need help to do this.

Think about...

What are you saying to keep yourself in this relationship?

What are the similarities between you and your husband and your father?... Not so much in personality, but in the way he treats you — and you treat him.

What are the differences?

THE HELPING ADDICTIONS

Question Seventy-Eight

What's the difference between codependency and compassion?

Com means to make common, and passion is a deeply felt zeal toward something or someone. Compassion is a powerful inclination to share deeply with another and to give support and aid to that person. Compassion is motivated by an intuitive understanding of another's situation and feelings. When we see someone else suffering, we feel a strong, natural tendency to help. Except in cases of extreme emergency when quick action must be taken, we also feel a compassion for ourselves and our own feelings. We normally take ourselves into account when we support another. Our motives are truly to help another person out of a troubled situation. And then to get back to our own lives.

When codependency is running rampant, we also are powerfully inclined to share, understand and help. This is why it's easy to confuse the two. The inclination in a codependent, however, feels more like a compulsion. We don't consider our own needs at all and often help at our own expense. And then we become angry when things don't go as we planned. Our hidden motive is often a deep need to control rather than to help. *Codependency is compassion gone haywire.*

Compassion offers a cool cloth to wipe a fevered brow when someone can't help himself.

Codependency pushes a cloth onto a brow that is not fevered at all and *insists* on wiping the brow of a person who has two good hands of his own.

Think about...

When was the last time you were compassionate rather than codependent?

Question Seventy-Nine

I just like to help people. I really do. My brother tells me to stop rescuing him, but I just love to help him. It makes me feel good. What does rescuing mean?

To *rescue* people in the language of Twelve-Step recovery programs means to help others without their consent or desire. It occurs when *you* the helper make the decision that help is needed. Notice what happens when you try to feed a baby who is ready to feed herself. She fights you for the spoon. She desperately needs and wants to feed herself. Feeding herself is her birthright.

The *helpee* may not truly *need* or *want* help or the kind of help we offer. But the *helper needs* to help anyway, regardless of true need or desire. Helping people can be an addiction when the *need to help becomes more important than the person in trouble*. See the question on codependency and compassion.

Think about...

Who do you rescue now?

How is this related to who you rescued as a child?

To whom do you turn when you're in real trouble?

Question Eighty

Does that mean that I can never help my family?

No. There is a fine line between helping and controlling. When we need help, we give nonverbal, covert clues or we ask outright. A healthy person, seeing a loved one floundering, responds in one of two ways. A response is expressed non-verbally with a hand held out in friendship and love, a gentle look, a tone of voice and through body language. A note of support, a phone call or a question, "Do you want some help?" verbally shows our concern.

To keep the help compassionate and supportive rather than codependent, we need first to check out whether we have the ability to help in this situation. We must be sure we have the energy to help at this particular time. Then we wait for the other's response rather than taking control and fixing the problem. When we do that, we make the other person feel helpless and out of control. We do not treat another's problem as our own, even a close or intimate person whose problem may at times spill out into our space.

Most importantly, we keep clearly defined limits for ourselves, the other person and the situation. We don't cross the boundary lines.

Think about…

Identify someone whose behavior you want to change. Go through the steps given.

Identify where you and the other person are.

Can you identify the boundary line?

How do you know when you are crossing the boundary line?

Question Eighty-One

I find it difficult to separate my own pain from my nine-year-old daughter's when it comes to her struggles, pain and rejection with her peers. Please help.

The pain that we feel around our children is the deepest pain there is. It is felt at the womb level. At the womb level, there is no separation between parent and child. Our child's pain is ours. This is one level of pain.

Another level is for our own Inner Child, aged nine, who is wounded. When our physical child reaches the age where we were most wounded, we must pierce our inner veil and press out our own pain.

A third level of pain is empathy. Empathy can form a bridge. But when we pity another person, we are really showing disrespect for that person. We don't respect our children when we give them the mothermessage that they are pitiable rather than lovable. This weakens them rather than building on their strengths.

We often think that our only pain comes from parents and siblings, but the truth is that much of our original pain comes from our peers. If we were ridiculed, humiliated and derided as children, we will need to deal with that pain also in recovery.

In the area of peer relations, only a peer can help. A parent's domain is not in the child's peer group. Seek help from school personnel on this part of the problem.

Question Eighty-Two

I have an eighteen-year-old daughter who is married. My problem is that she involves me in all her decisions and concerns after the fact. She tells me everything and more than I want to know. How do I separate myself from these concerns of hers?

This is a typical boundary violation. Allow her to experience the consequences of her own actions. Even though she's making her own decisions, she still wants your approval. For three times in a row, try not responding to what she tells you and see what happens.

When we are separating ourselves from mother, whose approval we need and want, we often want to share our lives but not ask for advice. What we as mothers need to practice at this point, is detachment.

When someone we love talks to us about her pain, we naturally become emotionally involved. The trick here is to express your feelings and your support for her efforts but not give advice. Young adults change radically in their twenties. She's not really asking you for advice. She's asking you to treat her as an adult who has the ability to make her own choices. (The choices don't have to be right all the time!)

If, after you've tried detaching and allowing her to experience the consequences of her choices, you still feel trapped, try to set up four to six counseling sessions with a therapist specifically trained in communication skills.

Think about...

When you listen to others, notice how often you secretly rebel.

Do you say what you mean and mean what you say?

Are you able to listen and support, yet refrain from offering advice or solutions?

Can you heed your own device?

Question Eighty-Three

I seem always to focus on the substance abusers in my family. How can I focus on myself?

Codependency is other-centeredness. When we are relationship addicted, our substance is other people. Focus on others distances us from our responsibility to ourselves. We must treat our obsession with our loved ones as the addiction that it is.

In relationship addiction, we become addicted to the drama of another person's life and problems. A good Al-Anon program is the best way I know to learn detachment. As codependents, we forget that we are people, too. Who is better equipped to help us than ourselves? Please, begin to treat yourself as well as you treat others. The Christian injunction is to love our neighbor as ourselves, not instead of. Remember that addictions replace true feelings, including those of love, peace and joy. We all deserve these feelings.

Think about...

Who is the main focus of your attention most of the time?

How are depriving yourself of the attention you need?

How could you give yourself more attention — today?

Question Eighty-Four

Do codependents ever let go of the need to make everything all right? To fix things for other people?

Yes. This is part of learning respect for yourself and respect for others. When we attempt to fix people, we arrange, set up, improve and determine what is best for other human beings. When we fix things for another person, we make certain assumptions:

1. The person is broken.
2. We have the power to fix the broken parts.
3. The person himself or herself has no power and no right to resolve problems in their own way and their own time.
4. God has no place in this scheme of things.

We are sure to get in trouble when we try to fix another person's life. We might have the best intentions in our heart, but in the end, our own heart may get broken. We need to be busy fixing our own. Remember the Prime Law of the universe:

1. There is a God.
2. It's not you.

Think about…

Who are you trying to fix?

Any luck?

What need in yourself are avoiding by trying to "fix"?

Question Eighty-Five

I do everything to please my family. They are my whole life. I'm isolated in my house. How do I escape? I'm so afraid of the outside world.

Codependents often feel a strong sense of inner isolation. We feel separate and set apart from others, as if we had been placed in quarantine.

This feeling arises partly out of faulty bonding but the main source is the ways in which we've been deeply shamed. Our inner shame creates a wall of isolation. We are terrified to come out into the light where we might be seen.

When we externalize this sensation, it is called agoraphobia. Agoraphobia is an irrational fear of open spaces — fear of leaving your home. One professional who works well with this phobia is a behavioral psychologist. Begin with a phone call.

Another way to approach the problem is through psycho-therapy. The underlying cause includes one of our deepest fears: a vulnerability which would expose our shame. There is no need to suffer with this any longer. You have a God-given right to your life and you deserve relief from your shame. Deep shame can be healed. Come out into the light and dance with your soul.

Think about…

Make a contract with yourself to take a first step toward healing your shame.

Question Eighty-Six

My eighty-three-year-old mother lives with my husband and me. I am an only child and there are no other relatives. She's a very depressed person and very difficult to live with. We want to put her in a senior citizen's home where she'd have some friends and activities. I have tremendous guilt feelings about this and yet I've decided this is the course of action to take. She's on a waiting list. My husband and I don't know how to tell her. I need help.

Wait til it's closer to her turn to be accepted into the home. Visit at least 4 or 5 homes for comparison so you'll be comfortable with your final decision. If possible, take her to visit the one you've chosen. Point out the positives but don't be too cheerful. It's difficult for people to change a life-style. Keep loving your mother. Take the approach that she's only changing residences and she still has some say-so about what happens to her. Be supportive, matter-of-fact and not condescending. The best thing to do is to get concrete advice from a local area agency on aging. Use this community resource to help tell your mother.

Do all that you can for your mother and then live your own life. Our parents gave us life and we have an obligation to live ours fully.

Question Eighty-Seven

My husband gets mad at me for all the work I do at our church. He says I'm neglecting myself and him. My back does hurt a lot, but I just don't pay attention to it. I don't want to be selfish.

The injunction is: Love one another as yourself, not instead of yourself. Don't do something for someone if it only fills your empty heart.

Hearts can grow to accommodate many other hearts. A full heart is a giving heart; an empty heart is hungry and never gets filled. Even by helping others. Don't do something for someone that you can't do. If we can't legitimately leave our children, husband or business to drive someone around, then they need to find another way to get where they want to go. Our friend or fellow church member needs to check out his/her own resources first. A healthy person will do just that. It is often the unhealthy codependent person who is demanding of the time and energy of others and resentful if someone truly can't help.

It is wise and charitable to allow other people in an organization to take turns at helping out and not always be the first to volunteer. Other people like to give, too.

Think about...

Examine the word "selfish" and its applications to your life.

Question Eighty-Eight

I'm doing well in my own recovery. I even feel happy lots of the time now. But my family of origin are suffering so, I feel bad for them. I feel so guilty that it interferes with my own work at times. Can you help?

When everyone in a family has suffered pain and terror together, a bonding occurs. This is a survivor-bonding, a bonding through pain. If one member escapes to recovery, it is natural to be concerned over the welfare of the others who did not escape. We feel, "Why should I alone get out of the pain and get relief, when the others are suffering so?" We feel as if we have abandoned our loved ones.

This is called Survivor's Guilt. The guilt comes from anxiety because I no longer share the same common enemy with my family. I have left them to their fate without trying to help. At the same time, my deepest fear is that I will relapse and fall once more into the darkness and despair of the family sickness.

Think about...

Have you ever felt guilty because you got better and someone else didn't?

What happened?

Write a letter to that person who is still in active addiction and/or codependency. Do not mail it.

Question Eighty-Nine

My life is all messed up. I'm on my fourth marriage, my children are in and out of relationships like revolving doors and I don't get along with them at all. I'm always afraid. Yet, when I look back on my childhood, I remember that I was very close to my mother. I'm still close to her, although my friends tell me she is mean to me. I don't see that. Something inside tells me that something is very wrong. Can you help?

The evidence of your life shows that your codependency is causing you a great deal of pain. Children who've been abused by a primary caretaker often form a fantasy-bond with their abusers. The child needs to be loved and valued desperately. She sees what she needs to see and avoids the pain of reality. The child creates an illusion of connectedness where there may be none at all. When the bond is one of pain, she blocks out the pain and puts in love. She doesn't recognize her needs for real love because she may never have known love at all.

In adulthood, then, we can't seem to let go of a relationship in which our needs are never met. We tell ourselves that the abuser really does love us and is punishing or neglecting us for our own good, to show us how to behave. We idealize the person and the relationship because we so deeply need the bonding, that we create a fantasy around it.

Think about…

Describe your relationship with your favorite parent. Can the bond be a fantasy bond?

Or is it real?

What do you remember from your childhood that assures you that you were valued by your parent(s)?

What were the sources of unhappiness for you as a child?

Question Ninety

I have trouble relating to my wife's moods. As soon as she walks into a room, I look at her face and I know something is wrong. I get that feeling in the pit of my stomach, my shoulders feel heavy and I get scared, just as I did as a child. What has this got to do with codependency? I was not raised in an alcoholic home.

A trigger for a codependent reaction is a person's face, especially a person to whom you've given a lot of emotional power. Our faces are our most expressive part. Moods are unresolved feelings. A trigger means that some outside stimulus has touched off feelings within us. The origin of these feelings usually lies in childhood. The feelings are already there, inside, like a deep pool — anger, fear, disappointment, shame, guilt.

Children from unhealthy homes are often visual and non-verbal and get very good at reading non-verbal signs of danger: body language. They are like hungry deer, standing still, head raised, body alert, listening, smelling and looking for signs of danger in the surrounding grass and trees. This is because verbal messages, which humans use, are not clear in these families. Also, Messages are often mixed.

If a child does check out with parents and ask for information, he might say, "Are you mad at me?" The answer might be, "No, don't be silly." "No, you're imagining that." "What's the matter with you? You're overly sensitive."

So the child learns not to say anything verbally, but instead to watch carefully, like a deer, for a parent's mood or mood changes. Faces are the clearest signs to read. A subtle change in eye muscle, mouth and other signs communicates to the child. Watch out. Danger. Drunk. Angry. Depressed. So when that child grows up, he learns to watch very carefully, without even realizing it, for any signs of tension or mood changes in anyone important to him.

That child also has learned not to ask for information, but to guess what is happening. In present adult life, the guess is sometimes wrong or the person misinterprets what is happening and so trouble begins. Sometimes, too, the Adult Child is correct in the "reading" of another person's emotions but the other person doesn't know it or doesn't want to deal with it right now. So we get the same reaction as we got in childhood. And we learn to "stuff" our feelings about it and to live in fear.

If you catch yourself noticing and reacting to another person's facial changes or mood changes that show up in body language, do check it out with the person, and believe what they say. Take it at face value. If something is wrong, it will come up again. Remember that you are not a child now and that your partner does not have the power of your parents of the past.

Simply ask your wife if she wants to share her thoughts or feelings with you. Tell her what you're feeling. Do not try to second-guess or read her mind. Discuss it with her. If she says nothing is wrong, then believe her and think about something else. Don't wait for the other shoe to drop. Don't obsess on it. If it is important, it will come up again. As an adult, you can deal with anything that comes up.

Think about...

When was the last time you tried to read another's mind?

PART FOUR

Sexual Abuse

Symptoms

Dissociation

Incest

SEXUAL ABUSE

One of the most severe, perhaps the most severe, forms of soulloss is sexual abuse. Sexual abuse of any kind results in the gravest of boundary violations. Sexual abuse is not about sex or sexuality, but about the abuse of power. It is about violence and inflicting pain. It is about power-over a helpless and innocent child. It is about humiliation and terror. The experience leaves huge, gaping holes in the soul of a child.

Question Ninety-One

I know what you mean about missing parts. I wonder what trauma I've had because I just feel incomplete. Tell me, what are some signs of sexual abuse?

SOME SIGNS OF SEXUAL ABUSE INCLUDE:

- Large gaps, even years, in childhood memories
- Disturbances in sleep patterns
- Eating disorders and other excessively compulsive behaviors
- Extreme shame reactions
- Delusions (mental ideas) that seem to have no basis in reality
- Night terrors
- Sleeping with a knife or club near the bed as a child or as an adult
- Sexual dysfunction
- No peace after sexual intercourse
- Rape in adulthood
- A pattern of conflictual relationships or no relationships at all
- Constant rage
- Gagging, excessive dry mouth
- Shooting pains or pressure in various parts of the body
- Self-mutilation
- Ideas about or attempts at suicide including passive suicide, that is destructive, life threatening behavior

If you have been in psychotherapy with a good therapist for two or more years and still feel that something is missing, that there's more here under the surface, and that you are not finished, sexual abuse *could be* undermining your progress.

It is very important to remember that none of these symptoms by themselves mean sexual abuse or incest for certain.

Question Ninety-Two

Sometimes I feel as if I am almost outside my own body watching and listening to myself. I may look like I'm interacting with someone. Yet I realize I want to yell, "Stop!" and really tell the person what I think. Also, when someone comes up behind me, to hug me or touch me, I flinch. I've had this feeling most of my life. I wonder if I have incest problems.

The feeling of being out of your body is called dissociation. Dissociation in and of itself is nothing to fear. It is a natural process and we do it every day. Notice when you drive a car and suddenly "wake up" to find yourself where you intended to go with no memory of how you arrived there. Dissociation under conscious control is one way that we enter an altered state of consciousness. This happens during deep meditation.

The dissociation which occurs in various forms during daily life in many homes is not of a healthy kind. Where chaos, disorder, disorganization, anger and fear reign, mild or major trauma occurs. The child, not able to deal effectively and efficiently with the environment in his home, will "space out." Parents often get reports of children "day dreaming" in school. This may be one explanation.

Involuntary dissociation as a response to trauma, causes a basic split between mind and body. This is not schizophrenic mental illness, although some incest survivors have been misdiagnosed. The unconscious process is a basic disowning, an invalidation of one's own private experience. To disown part of one's experience is to create a Disowned Child. We refuse to claim or accept as our own, a piece of our Inner Child. Events and the emotional meaning of events are blanked out of memory, like an alcoholic blackout, and repressed into an unconscious level.

You're on the right track. Dissociation is one indicator of sexual abuse. Something happens to us as a child that is too terrifying and painful to be faced and we cannot escape the situation. We cannot fight off the event nor can we run away from it. So we seek the only means of escape we have: we pull our souls out of our body so that we can't be hurt any more.

Incest is the *use* of a minor child to meet the sexual or emotional needs of a person whose authority is derived through *ongoing emotional bonding* with that child. This includes a parent, step-parent, priest, baby-sitter, brother or sister, mother's boyfriend, a teacher or a family doctor.

If we've lived through traumatic events as children, we may have been in a perpetual trance state. If we were dazed when the events happened, the mirror of our memory will be clouded and often blanked out. It's very important to get to the bottom of these events.

You need to seek professional help if you suspect sexual abuse. You will also want to check with others in the family where possible, for help in retrieving memories. Keep a memory log of what you do remember: what happened, who was involved, how old you were, how you felt then and how you feel now. Don't worry if your memories occur only in flashes or snatches. Look at pictures of you as a child. They may trigger possible associations, especially if you feel nothing at all. Notice who might have been taking the picture.

Whatever you do, talk to a trusted person about this and try to bring up more details until what happened becomes real and fairly concrete.

Question Ninety-Three

I have been in recovery for three years. I have been dealing with incest issues in therapy for the last year. I left my husband sixteen months ago and can't let go of the relationship. How can I find my own identity at the age of fifty-four? I think it will probably take as long as it takes. I am willing to go to any length to recover from this terrible trauma.

One of the most difficult things to face is the discovery of disturbing information at this stage of life. As difficult as it is, when memories surface, it is our Inner Child asking for validation. Our Inner Child asks us to make the past real, true and believable. After all, it is where her life began.

When we get information later in life, we need to grieve the years when we knew something was wrong but couldn't identify what it was. In the case of sexual abuse, we need also to grieve the lost innocence of our childhood.

For women, finding our own identity separate from husbands, marriage and children sets us free as nothing else does. For now, it is best to take one step at a time. When we first discover sexual abuse, we seem to lose faith in everything, self, others and especially God. The abused child confuses God with her abuser and loses her way. Keep up the good work and you'll find your way back to yourself.

I really like hearing that you are "willing to go to any length to recover." It's been my experience that those who say this with real honesty and determination are released from the prison of the past. When we see the daylight and feel the warmth of the sun and the rain, the tunnel of the past narrows more and more until it closes completely and we are at last free to move again.

Think about...

How far are willing to go in your own recovery?

PART FIVE

Return of the Soul: Personal Empowerment in Recovery

Grief and Forgiveness

Recovery and Beyond

RETURN OF THE SOUL:
PERSONAL EMPOWERMENT IN RECOVERY

Recovery means putting balance in our lives. It means calling our souls back home. It means personal empowerment and greening ourselves. In recovery, we will use our energy and soulpower to do the work that needs to be done. We empower ourselves every time we:

1. Say no to abusers and abuses, whether to ourselves or to any other living being, including Mother Earth.

2. No longer hurt, abandon or abuse ourselves and begin to count ourselves among those who matter.

The work of recovery is not easy and is filled with paradoxes. The way to begin is to make a commitment to ourselves. Any person, place or thing that comes into our lives must be examined for how it fits into our personal program. We can ask the question, "Does this move me further toward my recovery goals?" We must be willing to abandon old ideas and old ways and to move with the winds of change.

So often, we commit to a Twelve-Step Program without first dealing with the emotional issues underlying our addictions. We let go before we have looked at what we're letting go of. And our letting go becomes an empty gesture.

Our gift without our soul is barren. Our lives are a gift, and if we are to give ourselves and our lives over to the care of God as we understand God, we need to know the value of our gifting.

Emotional work must occur simultaneously with our spiritual work. The two supplement each other. When we are moving toward the goal of creating a healthy self to give to God, we are able to run lightly in the warm wind and feel the cool rain on our faces. We are able to dance with God. We are free to taste the gift of life itself. We smile as we welcome our souls home.

When you come to the edge of all light you know and are about to step off into the darkness of the unknown,

Faith is knowing one of two things will happen: There
will be something solid to stand on...or you will be
taught to fly!

GRIEF AND GRIEVING

Question Ninety-Four

I have just lost my mother. What does the normal grief process include?

The process is one of allowing our own death and choosing to be reborn, a letting go of the old, a cutting away of parts of ourselves, a divesting of energy and a final willingness to once more affirm life and invest in a new future filled with hope.

In the grief process, we become willing partners and are not frightened once we recognize the steps involved. It hurts but we don't panic. The process begins with naming who we've lost. I have lost my mother. My mother is dead. The next question is, what is the significance of your mother to you? We might answer, I have lost the person who was my biological mother. With her, I have lost my childhood. Whatever thoughts and feelings she and I had exchanged are also gone forever. I have lost what was in the relationship between us. And I have lost what was not between us.

The next phase is to acknowledge what Mother has given me to enhance my life and how she has diminished my life. We need to acknowledge further that we, she and I, will never be again. There will be no chance to rectify any mistakes on her part or ours. We need to mourn the lost chance, the diminishment and slowly and gradually to fill the need that only Mother could. Mother's inadequacies die with her. She will never have a chance to make amends to us. We must forgive her.

We can keep some of the precious parts and remember all that was between us that was good. We have a right to live on, even though that person has died. It makes no difference whether she has died physically or emotionally to us. We have a right to be better than our parents.

The last step is to restructure our personalities without that person in them. We rebuild our lives without them. Then and only then can we celebrate Mother's life as we mourn her death.

We cry tears for ourselves in this process. We also forgive ourselves. It takes one to five years to grieve a significant loss by death and quite a bit longer to grieve a loss by dysfunction.

Finally, we allow our grief to wash over us as the waves in the ocean wash over the shore and change it. When the waves leave the shore, the shore is no longer the same, yet its essence is still intact. The sand has shifted from the life of the waves to a life of its own. The sand has accepted its own life. The grief process is an affirmation of life.

Think about...

What was the most significant loss in your life?

How have you handled it? (No judgment)

Question Ninety-Five

When my father died five years ago, I felt no grief and did not cry at all. Two years later, I started crying but I think it was for myself. What happened?

It is quite common to have a delayed grief reaction, especially if you have come from a troubled home. You may have been angry at your father and unresolved issues got in the way of your very natural grief.

Loss is a part of life. We lose and we gain. We need to learn how to grieve our losses without experiencing paralyzing fear. In the process of mourning, we empty ourselves of the attachment to that which we've lost. When we grieve our parent, we grieve our idealized father, the father we never had, as well as the father we so desperately needed.

We grieve the very human man who happened to be our biological father. It may be that we did not like the person who happened to father us, and we need to accept that fact. We mourn the father that we need today, as an adult. We mourn our family and we mourn our childhood.

All of the hurts and pain, fear and anger, that we invested into our relationship with our parent come into play in the grief process. It doesn't matter whether the relationship was unhealthy or unhealthy.

When a parent dies, we stand alone on the island of life. This becomes clear as we allow the grief process to occur in a normal and natural way. If we are numbed out, unduly angry, do not allow our emotions full expression, then the grief goes underground. And we have a delayed grief reaction. Then the mourning is never expressed. It stays within us as a deep pool of pain. To that pool is added all the other losses in our lives.

When we grieve a current loss, we also grieve all of the losses that ever happened. We try to fill all of the holes within us. We feel like a bereaved, bereft child, an abandoned, orphaned child.

Recovery means crying old tears and going to the bottom of the bottomless well of pain. Recovery means recovering our natural selves in the process. Then we can finally speak in our own voice, hear with our own ears and see from our own eyes.

Think about...

For whom are you grieving today?

Questions Ninety-Six

I'm not sure I will ever be able to forgive my parents for my horrible childhood. It isn't fair, is it?

It isn't fair, but it is real. Remember that forgiveness is a process. It takes time and it takes surrender. This means that it does not occur all at once and then it is over. There are many elements in the process.

To forgive means to "stop feeling for or to stop feeling resentment against and to absolve from payment of". There is no way to make up for the past. There is no statute of limitations on parenthood, because the hands of parents reach far into the future.

Recovery means we are willing to be responsible for what we were not responsible for. It may have been our horrible childhood that caused our wounding but it is we who must now live our own lives.

In recovery, we see that even though our parents did the best they could, their best was not good enough for us. We now take away the power of our parents-of-the-past to influence our lives. We give up the inadequate parents that were and accept ourselves as our own best parent. We give the power for resources in our lives to ourselves. We take charge of our own lives. We take our life in our arms and embrace it in its fullness. We move on. We do not forgive our parents for their sakes, but for our own.

Think about...

Who will you never forgive?

Who do you want most to forgive?

Question Ninety-Seven

But I really am afraid to forgive. What if I forget and it happens all over again?

We cannot forget what was done, but our memories change our as our perceptions change. To forgive another does not mean to allow them to abuse us again, but only to let go of the BodyMind tension created within us by holding on.

The main thing needed in order to forgive is a mechanism for self-protection. This mechanism is called Boundaries. As Adult Children or codependents, we do not have such a mechanism. We were robbed of the growth of self-protection by our unhealthy family systems. For more, see question number twenty-two on Boundaries.

There are some things that are unforgivable, but when we forgive others for being unfair to us or letting their anger spill out onto our lives, we must also take away their right to do it again. We no longer allow others to abuse, neglect or ignore us. What we let go of is the tension we experience. What we gain is the ability to move on with our own lives. The more internal success we have in our own lives, the easier it becomes to let go of the past.

Think about…

Write down all the wounds from your childhood so that you won't forget them.

Then work on forgiveness in your own way in your own time.

Name two or three specific steps you might take as you work on forgiveness.

RECOVERY

Question Ninety-Eight

I guess that for some thirty-odd years, I have relied on someone else or some other opinion about anything and everything. At this point in my life, I feel like I'm going crazy at times, like a leaf in the wind, or someone who is abnormal. Can you help me?

The key in your question is that you have "relied" on others for "anything and everything." In the beginning of recovery, we need to ask the opinions of others because we have not been able to trust ourselves. The proof of this is that our lives have become unmanageable due to our illness. Once we have cleared away any insanities in our thinking, feeling and behavior, we begin to trust ourselves and our own intuition. When this happens, we may seek out the opinions of some people but the final decision is ours to make and we don't second-guess our decisions. Feeling out of control is the first step to the First Step. "I am powerless over ..." my feelings.

Get yourself to meetings, especially Adult Children of Alcoholics (ACOA) and begin to learn about the Twelve Steps to Recovery.

As you heal, you will begin to grow your own leaves and be able to take nourishment from your own soil.

Question Ninety-Nine

You talk about codependency and recovery. How can I recover? What are the steps?

There are different ways to recover. A first step would be to get into a Twelve-Step Program. Since codependency is a system based on lies and cover-ups, an important step is to break denial and tell the truth. It's such a relief to tell the truth!

Our denial system is very strong and very resilient. It has protected us well, for years, from the pain of discovery. Sometimes you will hear, "Through discovery to recovery." To recover means to discover your own, original, uncontaminated soul, that which is yours by birthright. The person you were before the codependency took over is waiting. You can return your soul to its rightful place within you. Remember what you sometimes hear: that which doesn't destroy us, makes us stronger. Build on that strength.

Think about...

Tell the truth about your codependency.

Question One Hundred

What is a Twelve-Step Program?

Twelve-Step Programs are essentially spiritual in nature. Since Alcoholics Anonymous began over fifty years ago, many other groups have formed. As more and more people realized that there is, indeed, an addictive process at work in our society, they began to seek help through a form that had already proven itself viable. There are literally hundreds of programs based on the Twelve-Steps of Alcoholics Anonymous. The focus of recovery varies with the kind of compulsions or addictions involved. But they all work!

A place to begin is to make a commitment to attend at least six meetings of Adult Children of Dysfunctional Families or Adult Children of Alcoholics. Codependents Anonymous is also appropriate. Try different ones until you find one that is comfortable for you.

Assuming that you are neither chemically dependent nor food addicted, and that, although you don't know what is wrong, you are sure that you need something more than your life is giving you now, just go there and listen.

The Twelve-Steps embody all of the basic principles involved in a viable, healthy life style. The main healing element in these groups is the internal knowledge and acceptance that by yourself you are unable to recover fully. The help that you need comes from God as you understand Him. It is emotionally, psychologically and spiritually healthy to learn to depend on a power greater than our own to help heal us.

It is also healthy and healing to be able later in the program to give back to the group what you have been given. That function is built into the program through sponsorship. A good Twelve-Step group to which you are matched can be a wonderful new family of choice. But a Twelve-Step group is not treatment in itself. It is not a course of therapy. It is a self-help support group designed to help you help yourself.

Think about...

With which Twelve-Step group will you begin?

Why?

Question One Hundred One

Is it possible to recover without a Twelve-Step Program?

Possible, yes.

Satisfying, maybe.

Joyful, no.

Question One Hundred Two

Explain how the Twelve-Step Program works in recovery.

The Twelve-Step Programs include all of the necessary elements of recovery from codependency. The program is essentially a spiritual one through which we become aware of the ways in which our attempt to solve problems in maladaptive ways has created its own set of problems. We learn to rely on God as we understand Him and our Twelve-Step group, as we were never able to rely on our parents. The therapeutic value of the program in and of itself is tremendous. If it is used in conjunction with individual psychotherapy treatment, the value increases.

There are three basic ways that people recover through Twelve-Step Programs:

1. Shared education and information.

2. Personal acknowledgment and expression of feelings.

3. Spiritual transformation.

By going to your first meeting, you are beginning to:

1. Break denial, stop blaming others and take responsibility for our own behavior.

2. Fill the need for a human witness to our truth and our pain.

3. Our story becomes real as we tell it.

4. As our story becomes real, we begin to deal with our past.

5. Other people may have reactions to our codependent story, thus we connect our experience to that of other people. We let out our secrets.

6. We normalize our experience by hearing the stories of others.

7. When people listen to us as if we are important and as if what you say does make a difference, it gives credence and confidence to us and our story. This time we are not told to sit down and shut up, that the adults are more important than the children, and that there is no time for us now. There is time.

8. We are accepted exactly as we present ourselves and for exactly who we are at that moment.

9. When we accept and begin to "work on" the steps themselves, they provide a wonderfully sound guide for self work, self acceptance and self confidence.

10. As we think about this new set of principles and guide lines by which to live, it may be the first time in our lives that we have a choice about how we are to live.

11. Another healthy practice is the tradition of rotating leadership at meetings. There are no authorities, only peers. Each time we speak publicly, we hear ourselves. We respond emotionally to the material and we are supported by the responses of others in the group.

12. We are being heard and counted. We are standing up for ourselves in our life situation.

Each meeting begins and ends in the very same way each time and the format stays the same. This provides predictability for members. The Program gives a common language for all, unlike the dysfunctional family system. By sharing a common language, people bond with one another. There is always spontaneous sharing by the members, whether or not there is an outside speaker. This provides validation for members. We can check out outer reality with other people in an environment that is supportive but realistic.

A main tenet of the Program is that I, personally, am accountable for my own actions. The causes of my illness do not matter in today's reality. However, people feel safe in these meetings because of the rules of confidentiality and anonymity.

Finally, in relinquishing outer power to God and our group, we gain internal power to effect change in our own lives. This remains one of the paradoxes of the Program.

Question One Hundred Three

Is it really possible to achieve balance in my life?

Recovery means not depending on a crisis to feel alive. As children, we become so used to constant crises in our lives that as adults we often create chaos in order not to feel bored. We become addicted to the rush of adrenaline that accompanies a crisis situation and we feel at home in a storm.

Balance is not a static state, but, rather consists of managing our lives and weighing alternatives. In order to stabilize our experience, we move freely between thinking, feeling and acting. It is indeed possible to achieve balance once we face our fear of it. When chaos is all we have known, we must learn that balance is not boredom and freedom is not frightening. We stop crying alone in the dark closet and we learn to rejoice and dance in the sunlight.

Think about...

How do you use a crisis to feel alive?

When there is neither a present crisis nor a pending one, do you feel anxious... incomplete... fearful?

Question One Hundred Four

How do I recover from codependency without leaving all my friends and family, even though they are the ones that make me codependent? I'd die if I were not loved!

We don't necessarily need to leave all of our friends and family when we recover. We can separate out our relationships, one from another, and determine which ones are codependent and in what ways they are so. If we remove all of the dysfunctional people from our lives, we may find ourselves alone on a hilltop.

We all want and need to be loved. However, it is the price we are willing to pay for being loved that causes the trouble. It is natural and healthy to want to please those we love, but we as codependents we tend to abandon ourselves in favor of others. To please others at our own expense is a codependency issue. A relationship is healthy if there are clear negotiations so that both people can be satisfied.

There's nothing wrong with wanting people to like us, but it is the unspoken, *at any cost*, that keeps us codependent. When we begin to feel angry at those we love, we know we're losing ourselves and we panic because we think we're going to die! The bottom line here is: Recovery from codependency is the willingness to abandon and to be abandoned, if that's what it takes.

Think about…

When do you cross the line?

How far are you willing to go?

Question One Hundred Five

Why can't I get out of a relationship that I know is wrong for me? I leave for four days and the pain drives me back. This happened after I got sober. When I drank, I could leave relationships.

Sobriety is more than not drinking. Sobriety allows us to see what we blocked out, to hear what we stopped up. What we see and hear is our own soul, struggling to be born, striving to live. We want desperately to express the essence of ourselves. Once the drug-dependency leaves, we are often left with other-dependency. We must go through the black, soundless tunnel of aloneness to be born free, maybe for the first time.

Have you ever been out in nature and felt the freedom, the aloneness, that turned into oneness? This is a taste of rebirth. We must walk, swim, crawl through the "tunnel of abandonment" to see, hear and know our own spirit.

Think about…

Notice the feeling of oneness the next time you are out in nature.

How can you carry that feeling into your daily life?

Question One Hundred Six

I have a terrible problem with a recent romantic breakup. How do I break this horrible attachment and stop clinging to something that will probably no longer be?

You stop by cutting off your internal mental and emotional interaction with the person. The ways in which we continue an interaction with a person who is no longer with us are to imagine how he'd feel, what he'd say and what he'd do when something happens in our lives. Then, based on his response, we create a whole play. We create scenarios and repeat them over and over and over. We call this The Play Remains the Same. We become obsessed with the imaginary dialogue. And we become obsessed with the accompanying feelings. Sometimes we even become addicted to the feelings, seeking them out. If we find a new partner, we can repeat the play. The Play Remains the Same, only this time the players change.

We carry this out in many areas of our lives. If we're invited out, we say, "Oh, no, I don't want to go alone," meaning, "I'd go, if only Bob were here to go with me."

If the obsession goes on too long and is too intense, we may be experiencing left-over feelings from past abandonments.

When another person does not want a relationship with us, we are, in fact, rejected. We feel very strongly that old hole in the pit of our stomach. There's an empty, black space that's filled only with darkness, coldness and pain. A void. No one is there. So we once more feel like that child we were when we were first abandoned. If our abandonment occurred at age three, then we will feel three years old rather than the chronological age that marks our life experience. When we feel the hole of abandonment, we know we are close to our Inner Child. A beginning Inner Child workshop is a good place to start.

Think about…

How are you repeating the same play again and again in your relationships?

Who are the actors and how do they act?

What is the script?

Question One Hundred Seven

Four years after my divorce, I find myself as dependent on my ex-husband as I was when we were married. How do I stop?

Become emotionally divorced. Begin in small ways by doing things for yourself rather than asking him to help you.

A divorce involves many levels of recovery. There are the physical separation, legal and financial aspects, parenting issues, social losses such as family and friends and the emotional pain of abandonment and rejection.

When we married, we did not expect to find ourselves in a position of being forced to let go of our dream of love and commitment. We did not expect to find ourselves in a place of deep grief. If we do not grieve, we are holding on. Know that grieving and letting go are followed by restructuring our lives and getting to know ourselves. Healing will come.

Think about...

How can you become emotionally divorced from a loved one?

Question One Hundred Eight

How can I articulate my feelings to someone who is not here physically? My ex-boyfriend lives in another state but I have some feelings that came up after the relationship ended.

This is called unfinished business. Write four letters, not to be mailed out but to be kept and processed by you.

The first one should be a dumping of all the feelings you can think of. Be as unfair as possible. Don't see his side at all.

The second one should be to yourself. Experience all of your own feelings about what happened. Include your anger at yourself for allowing certain things to happen, your hurt and regrets. All of it.

The third letter should be one of self-forgiveness. Forgive yourself for hurting yourself and understand that you acted and felt out of your needs at the time.

The last letter should be a forgiving good-bye to him. Tell him all the truth, your part and his. Tell what you have learned from the relationship. Say good-bye finally. And then do something really nice for yourself.

Do not mail these letters. They are to be used as a mirror of yourself. It may take up to a year to complete the letters. If you need to write a letter to be mailed to him, do it from a position of strength, after you have worked out the feelings to your satisfaction. When this is completed, you will feel a sense of freedom and joy and you'll be able to spread your wings and soar over the pain.

Think about…

Name the people in your life who need letters.

Write your own series of letters. Who will you write to first?

Question One Hundred Nine

It seems as if I have no room for me, whoever that is, inside of myself. I really don't know who I am. All I keep thinking about is my parents' saying, "Don't do this! Do that!" and "I'll show you who's boss!" Can you help me?

This is a classic case of an adult children growing up to fight our parents' endlessly within ourselves. No one wins and there is no chance to find out more about ourselves and how we would feel, think and act, if we didn't hold our parents inside.

There are ways we can use the inner voices we seem to hear to focus our attention and direct our energies. It is helpful to separate out these voices, one from another. They are like audio cassette tapes that play messages to our inner ears and keep us stuck in the past. The voices come from memories, fantasies and imagination. Some voices speak out of our past, some organize our present lives and others direct our future actions. Try to identify each voice.

There is our "mother voice:" things mother said or implied by her actions...even what mother wanted to say or would have said if...

There is our "father voice:" things father said or implied by his actions...also what father wanted to say or would have said if...There are the voices of brothers, sisters, aunts, uncles, priests, ministers, teachers, friends, parents of friends. There are so many voices that we find it hard to distinguish among them.

A way to begin working with this inner dialogue is to get a large piece of paper and a pen. Begin writing down as many as you can of the random thoughts in your head, as quickly as you can. It's o.k. if you miss some.

Once you have filled three sheets with phrases, sentences and words, begin to identify who might have said what.

Hearing the voices may cause you some shame and guilt, but do it anyway. It is now o.k. to talk back to these voices. Allow your feelings to come up and write those down, too. Work with the voices by putting the separate ones on three-by-five cards. You can shuffle these and arrange them in any order you want. Begin to discard those you don't believe in, no longer want and those which do not work for you in adult life. You can tear them up, burn them or scribble over them with black marker. Do this with feeling.

When the voices of the others have been identified and sorted out, begin to create your own. This is done by quieting yourself. Use a candle or some other focusing device. Quiet yourself by deep breathing. When you feel calm and peaceful, listen. Just empty yourself and listen. The tiny, small, quiet voice you hear is your own. Begin to listen carefully to that voice when it whispers to you. It will whisper in dreams, in daydreams, whenever you are quiet, still and receptive.

You will know this voice is yours by its quiet tone. The other voices are noisy, strident and demanding. Begin to be grateful for your own voice and to respect it. Your voice is a vital part of who you are. Celebrate it.

Question One Hundred Ten

How can I get my father's voice out of my mind? I keep going over and over the same old stuff with him, even though he is dead. I want to be able to hear only my own voice.

Try a Voice Dialogue. Sit in a quiet place where you won't be disturbed. Sit quietly for about fifteen minutes. See your father sitting across from you — or you can visualize him in any familiar position. You can use photographs of him to focus your attention. Remember exactly what your father tells you. Hear his voice again. Unlike the incident that really happened in your past, this time you are to answer him back in your language of today.

You have permission to shout, cry, stamp and wave your arms around as you feel moved to. You especially have permission to talk back to your father and to say the things that you never were allowed to say as a child. Allow your father to talk back if you wish. Continue the process.

This time you are in control of the situation. You can make your father do anything you want him to do, even apologize to you for his wounding of you.

When you and your father are finished arguing, create an appropriate ending to the situation.

You can say:
"We are finished for now. But I'll be back when I need to."

"I am not finished with you. I still feel (anger, fear, resentment) for you. I will meet you again. On my terms."

"We are finished forever. I need to tell you good-bye and I wish you well."

"We are finished. I will never forgive you for what you did to me. Good-bye forever."

"I forgive you. I forgive myself. I love you. I love me. Amen."

Question One Hundred Eleven

Once I find my own Inner Child, how do I take care of him? How can I become my own parent and empower myself?

To empower ourselves, we need to recognize, acknowledge and heal the wounds of childhood. We must examine the rules and principles by which we have lived to determine whether these still work for us as adults and then we can decide on a set of principles, values and beliefs that we will abide by. Be aware that what this means is that we become our own authority and take full responsibility for our choices.

This is a tall order but much of the heart of recovery lies in this area. It is well worth the pain and effort to be free and self-determining. If we want to go to Santa Fe but we are on a train headed for Detroit, we'd better get off quickly!

To become our own best parent, we need to create a healthy home for our adult selves and a safe place to be.

Think about…

What are the dysfunctional rules you used to live by?

How can you change those now?

Question One Hundred Twelve

What is a healthy home?

A child is like a plant. If we are given lies to replace love and if we are given abuse instead of attention, we become weakened and diseased. With the right amount of sunshine and water, we bloom. People are more adaptable and resilient than plants and we try to explain away the horrors and pain of childhood toxins. Often, however, in spite of our best efforts, we absorb these toxins and become sick.

In healthy homes, children get all the love and attention they need. They may not get everything they want, but appropriate limits are set. These children are not deprived and there is enough nurturing and guidance to go around. People who live in healthy homes are expected to be honest, open to change and flexible. Bodies are nourished with healthy food. Minds are seeded with open and positive thoughts. Encouragement is freely given. Good energy flows freely throughout the family. Home is a safe place to grow, explore and to experiment in the world.

Today, as adults, we can create such a home for ourselves. To do this, we learn to treat ourselves as if we were our own natural child. We do not criticize, ridicule or punish ourselves as we learn. We don't have to be perfect. If we encourage ourselves in our efforts and let our love show in our eyes when we look in the mirror, we will see a growing, healthy person.

Think about…

How could you provide for yourself a healthy home, physically?

Socially?

Emotionally?

Spiritually?

What changes do you have to make to provide this for yourself?

Question One Hundred Thirteen

What do you mean by a safe place? I've never known safety in my life.

Safety is a basic emotional need. We cannot survive emotionally without feeling safe. When we are unsafe, a part of our soul leaves our body. Our soul knows that we cannot grow in an atmosphere of veiled danger, with people who lack knowledge and skills of living with emotional aliveness.

Safety is related to trust. If we can't trust our environment which consists of the people around us, then we can do nothing but watch, listen and search for signs of trouble.

If we have lived as children on the rim of a volcano, with constant threats to our physical, emotional or sexual development, our BodyMindSoul is conditioned to danger. Our BodyMindSoul automatically reacts as if the danger is still present. We become hyperalert to our environment and hypersensitive to other people. We are defensive and we need protection. We are not venturesome or creative.

This is why your soul left. You sent it into exile because reality was too painful for you. You now need to seek it, retrieve it and welcome it back.

As adults in recovery, first we create a safe place in our minds and then we surround ourselves with friendly, healthy people who are interested in our well-being. In a healing place, we heal. We get off the rim of the volcano and walk by the beautiful sea. Gulls play and waves wash our feet. We laugh in the morning sun. Our soul is safe.

Think about......

Where in your adult life do you feel most safe?

Where, if anywhere, did you feel most safe as a child?

Question One Hundred Fourteen

I've been in recovery from alcohol and drug dependency for the last four years. My husband put together three years last week. Although he has been sober for three years, in the last few months, he has slipped twice, drinking a weekend each time. My question is, how do I not monitor his program and still allow myself to care for him? I have difficulty with balancing this situation.

This is a common problem for recovering couples. Recovery changes the balance in a marriage. Each partner must focus on his or her own recovery issues. We must be patient with ourselves, as well as with our partner. It is hard to see someone we love suffer. Sometimes doing nothing is the hardest lesson to learn. But you are right: it is a matter of balance.

Without working his Program, you might say something like, "I noticed that over the last few weekends, you have had slips. I'm concerned about you because I love you. I'd feel better if you talked to your sponsor about it." And then drop it! And go to your own meetings. Go about your own business.

Think about...

What Step are you working on now?

Question One Hundred Fifteen

Al-Anon tells me to detach with love. I don't know what that means. What is detachment?

Al-Anon has done a great job teaching the concept of detachment. To detach from someone does not mean to stop caring or to stop loving. To detach means to separate the person from her behavior. It is really a gentle release of the other person onto her own path. It is allowing another person to make his own mistakes without your intervention.

A second part is to focus less on the other person's feelings and behavior. What they do, say, think or feel is truly separate from our own experience. We are not responsible for their actions. People do not necessarily feel just the same, even in similar situations. To detach is to admit that the outcome is not in our hands. To release is not to judge but to allow another human being her own soul.

It is to fear less and to love more.

Think about......

Can you identify a person in your life that you need to release?

List your own behaviors that do not allow you to detach from that person.

What is your secret fear?

Question One Hundred Sixteen

I don't understand the idea of letting go. Let go of what, I ask you?

Significant damage is done when we hang on to the persons, places or ideas we think will fix us or ones that we feel compelled to fix. We seem to like to hang on to our illusions and our delusions, the hurtful words people have said to us, those things we think will never abandon us or betray us and yet we get betrayed again and again. How many next times can there be?

We need to let go of many things, including tension in our bodies, illusions (mental pictures) of romance or perfect parents and delusions (false thoughts) that life will always be fair and that nothing bad will happen if we are good people.

Letting go is the opposite of holding on. It is an open hand rather than a closed fist. It is smoothing out a frown to replace it with serenity. It is a deep, abiding trust in a power greater than ourselves. It is a deep, sure knowledge that we don't have to do it all ourselves, and it is allowing other people to have their part in the events of our lives. Letting go means that God, as we understand Him, runs the world and that some things are not our business.

Letting go means releasing our ego investment, the idea that we are all powerful. Ego, the all important King Baby, the narcissistic person inside of us does not really run the show. Letting go is releasing all the parts of our lives that we can't really control anyway. We only fool ourselves. Letting go means taking responsibility for only our own small parts in the larger scheme of things and in our relationships. It means knowing that we personally don't always have to do something but we only have to be something, a human being.

Letting go means knowing that to be human is to be fallible and sometimes frail and being humble enough to admit this and say a simple, "I'm sorry." It also means knowing our own strengths and never forgetting our own dignity and worth as human beings.

When we let go we don't abdicate responsibility but we recognize that we can't control the outcome of every situation. When we get into a car, it is impossible to predict the outcome of our drive. We may or may not have an accident. Our part is to drive the car as competently and ably as we can and to stay alert. Once we do that, we trust God to decide the outcome of our journey.

We hope that nothing bad happens and we trust that if it does, we can handle it.

Letting go means pedaling our own bike and leaving our destination up to God. Letting go means putting our energy into achieving recovery instead of harboring rage. If we do this, we achieve self-acceptance instead of self-abuse and peace rather than perfectionism. It's such a relief!

Think about…

What do you need to let go of in your life today?

How will you let go?

Question One Hundred Seventeen

Because I have been codependent most of my life, I am not sure if I can recognize a healthy relationship. How will I know when I'm in a healthy relationship?

A relationship is healthy and growing when it's easy to love, and the demands are few. When it feels good and natural, not intense or high, and when it's fun, it is healthy. A relationship is growing when there is substance and safety in the feeling between the two of you and when your partner is your close friend. When the two of you can fight without bitterness and love without clinging. When love doesn't hurt and partners take responsibility for themselves as well as for each other and when the bond of love is pleasure rather than pain, you know you're on the right track. You can relax into it when you more of your best self with the other person rather than without her.

A healthy relationship feels peaceful, is mutually respectful and honors the love between you. When you can walk together, shoulders touching, arms linked, hearts in tune, with shining faces turned toward the future, you know you are both healthy and growing.

Think about...

Which of the above elements are in your present relationship?

Which need improvement?

Question One Hundred Eighteen

Is it possible to ever be completely independent? I believe that being autonomous and intimate is what most healthy relationships are. But it seems contradictory to me. How do you act when you are in a serious relationship?

We are all interdependent. We depend on each other and on our earth to sustain life. Intimacy is not a state to move into and stay in, but is rather a dance to learn. To dance with a partner means to step closer and farther away in response to your own inner rhythms and your partner's signals. You need to learn the same dance steps, so you will be in sync.

This is one of the many paradoxes inherent in life, living and recovery. A paradox is a clash of opposing and seemingly mutually exclusive forces: autonomy and intimacy, for example. Our willingness to move to the music of the dance and to risk conflict is what creates real and lasting change. The process is painful, arduous and dangerous. Codependents find this easy to do externally but difficult to do emotionally.

When we decide to rise to the challenge, we discover that the dance is fun. When we have fought and won, we no longer think in rigid, black and white terms. We have created changing colors in our lives and new steps to an old dance.

Think about...

Talk with your partner about the dance steps the two of you do now.

How could your dance be improved?

Question One Hundred Nineteen

You talked about spinning thinking earlier. Is there recovery from this kind of problem?

Yes, there is. Recovery has to do with being willing to deal with your feelings. One technique is to defocus from the problem temporarily and to focus instead on your feelings about what is happening. Rather than confronting our feelings as part of the problem when we are addicted to spinning, we begin to flail around obsessively. We have learned that it is not safe to feel or to acknowledge our feelings, much less to express them. When we express our feelings to a safe person, we begin to take the next step, which is to discover or create solutions to the basic problem.

A way to begin is to first know that you are spinning. Recognize your self-talk. The next thing to do is to stop everything. Take a few deep breaths. Drink a glass of water. Think of something else for a moment.

When you are ready, write down the basic problem in one or two sentences or phrases. If there is more than one problem, write each one separately. Then sit quietly for a moment and allow your feelings to surface. Write all of your feelings down, just as they occur, whether or not they make logical sense. Do not censor your reactions. Sit quietly. If and when the thoughts begin again, start over with deep breathing. Drink some water.

Do not attempt to solve the problem yet. Talk to your therapist or to a close friend. Hold off discussing the actual problem. Stick to your feelings about the problem first. There is no rush. The problems has been with you for a very long time. Some problems have no solutions, but must be accepted. Try to distinguish by saying the Serenity Prayer. "God, grant me the serenity to accept what I cannot change, the courage to change what can be changed and, (most importantly) grant me the wisdom to know the difference." Some solutions will come to you after you have dealt with your feelings about it.

Each and every time you begin to "spin", take the above steps until the habit is broken and you can think again.

Question One Hundred Twenty

What is the normal state after we have overcome codependency? How can we tell if we've arrived and are no longer sick?

If we think we've overcome codependency, we probably haven't. One criterion of health, however, is the ability to set a realistic, manageable goal, including emotional ones, based on our own life interests and to feel great about ourselves and our accomplishments when we reach that goal. Another indication is we have no second thoughts about our decisions or ourselves and we don't continue to go over and over the same problem once we've arrived at a solution. We know we are healing and growing when we are able to view our lives realistically yet positively. We own our own lives and we do not give other people our inner power. When we cry all our tears, laugh at ourselves and playfully thumb our nose at the world, then we know we are living life as it was meant to be lived.

Think of our selves and our lives as a circle. Our center is God and our personal soul or essence, that which activates movement in us. Around the center are spokes. Each spoke is an aspect of our life: spiritual, emotional, physical, financial, work, family, our primary relationship, children, friendships. We tend to forget or to put last priority on the emotional and spiritual spokes. When some of the spokes are missing, the wheel falters and we get off balance.

Every day we go to sleep, wake up, take a shower, pay our bills, do affirmations and have a quiet conversation with our inner soul force. Then we go off to earn our living. No one thing is more important than any of the others. Balance is the key. And achieving balance is an ongoing process.

Think about...

What one thing can you do today to commit to your recovery?

Draw the circle of your life, identifying each spoke.

Which spokes are you most likely to neglect and let collapse?

Question One Hundred Twenty-One

How come I am in recovery and am still unhappy. Why is this so?

We can look at recovery as a three-stage process. Try to identify which stage you are experiencing now.

PRIMARY STAGE

This is an early, most painful phase. In this part, we are letting go, releasing everything we've ever known, including a life style developed around our addictions. Grief is our constant companion during this part of the process.

We deal with our addictions in layers, one at a time. The first to go are chemical addictions: alcohol, other drugs, sometimes nicotine. But other addictions rise up to fill the void: eating, relationship, spending. During this stage, the addiction is like a monster making a last-ditch effort to hang on.

At the same time, we feel deep within us the small voice of our healthy side trying to be heard. The battles rage within our bodies, minds and souls. The addict within keeps trying to seduce us and intimidate and conquer us. We make a kind of bargain and crawl along, but we often feel deprived. Life hardly seems worth the living.

There are actual chemical changes taking place as we empty ourselves of the toxins produced by our surface addictions.

MIDDLE STAGE

We limp along to the middle stage. Here we recognize our family of origin issues. We realize that we really do have choices, but we don't know how to make them. We live in a fog of chaos, and our natural self is still shadowy. The problem is that the implications of these choices are driven home to us in often painful ways. We cannot recognize our natural selves. We are unpredictable to ourselves. We need to learn an entirely new life-style based on new principles. Choice means giving to gain. We must give up what isn't working and make fresh, new choices every day. The balance beam is hard to walk.

FINAL STAGE

The struggle continues until we reach the final stage of recovery in which we truly experience our real selves and we begin to trust that self. We feel the freedom that our daily choices give us. We feel the real joy of giving back to others what we've received. We are no longer afraid of ghosts that walk in the night. We face them all.

We no longer say, "What if something happens: who will help me?" We now say, "When something happens, my Higher Power and I will be able to handle it."

We have surrendered. When we doubt ourselves and our perceptions, we call upon our inner strengths and our outer resources in friends and other people who can and are willing to help. Our program of recovery has become a vital part of our personality and the principles by which we live are ours.

The cycle of addiction has been changed to an open-ended system. We no longer spin around, but are we-centered.

Think about...

What stage of recovery are you in now?

How do you know this?

What is the most difficult part of this stage for you?

What, in this stage, makes you feel good about yourself?

Question One Hundred Twenty-Two

How long does it take to fully recover from codependency?

Recovery is a lifelong process. We have all the time we need. We have the rest of our lives. There is no need to hurry or to hassle ourselves. Recovery includes a remediation process, a therapeutic process, a healing process and a restorative process. Note the word "process". Recovery is ongoing.

During the remediation process, we delve into our past to re-experience past traumas in order to create a different, more healthy outcome.

We learn what actions to take in order to do the healing work in the therapeutic part. While we are healing, we allow ourselves to mend without interference from the critical judge who sits inside of us.

The last process is a restorative one during which we bring some order to our lives and pick up the shattered pieces. The whole process takes from eighteen months to four years. Not all of the work needs to be done in formal psychotherapy, but psychotherapy is most helpful and often necessary.

It is important to have some guidelines for recovery but we need not to overwhelm ourselves. Be patient, kind and understanding. You have all the time you need.

Think about...

Are you willing to go through all the processes to recovery?

If you have moved through one or more of these processes, describe your reactions to it or them.

Question One Hundred Twenty-Three

What is a codependent attack?

When we choose recovery, we no longer live a codependent life style. We no longer become physically sick and emotionally devastated or depressed. We live more in the middle ranges and bring excitement to our lives in constructive ways. But relapse does happen.

A codependent attack is an emotional relapse. Relapse in chemical dependency is clear: we pick up the first drink and our insides change. Relapse in codependency is also signaled by change.

There is a recurrence of the feelings, thoughts or behaviors we had when we were living our former life style. The old feelings and thoughts may come on in subtle ways and we realize we're skating on thin ice — or there may be a sudden plunge into the icy waters of codependent reactions.

We don't have to do recovery perfectly, but each of us has a life area where our codependency shows up. It can be seen in work, relationships and other areas where we are vulnerable. Jean may become immediately obsessed in a new relationship with a controlling man and feel depressed. On her job, Mary may begin to think old thoughts like, "No matter what I do, I can't finish all my work. What do they want from me anyway?" Jim notices that he is beginning to overeat again.

We may feel our chest tighten, our breath may become shallow and short and our stomach knots up like it used to. We are suffering emotional flooding. When our bodies are numbed out and our heads are spaced out, we are in the grips of emotional paralysis. Either state is perilous.

There are times we need to be on the alert for signs of a codependent slip. Times to watch for relapse signs are times of change. When we know we are off balance or tired either physically or emotionally, we need to check our internal climate. We need to watch for times when we feel lost, fragile or weak and when our boundaries begin to blur, we need to be alert.

Times of vulnerability occur when we are in early recovery, especially during the first year. When life experience creates uncertainty and brings fear, it is time to be careful. When we suffer a major loss such as a job firing, divorce or a death, when we feel failure, anger and desperation and have a stronger-than-normal feeling response, we need to stop and re-evaluate our recovery program and our commitment. If we find ourselves in an abusive situation which reactivates previous experience or we find ourselves clinging, avoiding or denying reality, our insides change. We are more open to a relapse and likely to slip off our chosen path into codependency at these times.

Certain people, events and situations can cause a codependent attack. People who are familiar to us in that they remind us emotionally of parents, siblings or others in our unhealthy past are unsafe. Those who are critical, clinging, alcoholic, pitiful or unavailable are sure to trigger an inside change.

Life events which include drastic change like falling in love or the birth of a new baby are situations to watch. We also need to be on the alert for situations which are emotionally familiar to our old ways in which we begin to notice that we are neglecting ourselves, feeling drained or strained, not feeling good about ourselves or feeling crazy, out of control or numb.

We may notice that the more out of control we feel, the harder we try to control our external world. This is a sign that our codependency has become active again. When we get even one of these signals, we need to stop and be kind, gentle and soft-spoken to our new selves, as we would to a good friend of ours who was troubled. When souls return, they need to be made welcome.

Recovery is not linear but occurs in a spiral fashion. Recovery is a stained glass mosaic. It is a mandala of love. As we get better, the attacks get shorter and are less intense. We are able to recognize the signs of codependency much more quickly. What used to be a major illness becomes the twenty-four-hour flu.

BEFORE YOU LEAVE...

A Personal Message from Dorothy

We have finished our work together and it's time to close the book for now. I have spoken to you about the deepest essence of yourself, which I call soul. The loss of soul occurs in bits and pieces throughout the course of a lifetime, through deprivation, disease and trauma. Often this begins early in life. When we have had a relationship with someone significant and have been subjected to emotional devastation and betrayal, we withdraw from conscious reality. We become essentially dead to the world. Later unhealthy emotional attachments produce the same state of being. Surgery, accidents and other shocks to the system leave us feeling beside ourselves and spaced out.

My own loss of soul occurred many years ago, in a time I can barely remember. I knew something was wrong when I became uncomfortable, dissociated, with a woolly feeling inside that I could only call confusion. Outwardly, I had gone on in my life beyond my early experiences, but there was a prolonged numbness and a strange sensation that part of myself was missing. Had been missing since ... the event. In my case, the dysfunction in my family intensified with the marriage (the event) of my oldest brother when I was nine. When he married, the ball was passed to me. I began to die a little then. A bit of my soul left, not to return until I was about thirty years old. The ball was my mother and her neurotic needs and my distanced father. I was a Prisoner of War in my parents' marriage battles. The ball was heavy for me but I carried it well into my adulthood.

There is a progression to soulloss. As a child, the first time we were discounted, put-down, betrayed, neglected, deprived, abandoned, criticized or abused, we began to lose a bit of our deepest essence, our soul. When disease or accidents happen, we lose a bit more.

We begin to internalize the feelings and self-image that is a result of emotional scarring. Then we begin to change into a false, codependent self in order to adapt ourselves to our environment. We develop a tolerance to abuse and pain. Blocks of ice begin to form within our internal system. The blocks of ice cover the flame of passion and it begins to burn lower. Sometimes by adulthood, it is only an ember.

The way to recognize soulloss in myself is not by the events I've suffered but by feeling-symptoms. A partial list of feeling-symptoms is in Appendix B.

Once we recognize soulloss, we can begin the process of calling our soul back home. To *Call Our Soul Home,* we need to take our healing seriously…to make our recovery top priority. Healing does not mean instant cure but it does mean a whole-ing of ourselves in an ongoing process called *Living our Lives. Whole-ing ourselves IS life!*

CALLING SOUL HOME

I will share with you some of the healing tools that have been successfully tested on myself and with other people. As with all of the material in this book, you have my full permission to take what you need and discard what doesn't work for you. But a word of caution is in order here. If something doesn't work at one point in time, it may work later on in recovery.

The first condition for this work of recovery is safety. We need to create a relatively safe place for ourselves. A witness, friend or partner helps but is not necessary for all the parts to return. Often we experience a spontaneous return. When the conditions of living become safe both internally and externally, the soul will naturally want to come home and often will return of its own accord. You need do nothing in this case but keep abuse out of your life.

Even small acts of self-validation can be a part of the soul return process. One woman who allowed herself to be forced into an unwanted business partnership with her husband simply had new business cards and stationery made. She had the words "and associates" removed. Since these words symbolized that partnership for her, it was an act of freedom. She burned the old cards in a ritual fire, and offered prayers of release and forgiveness for herself and her husband.

Another woman who had a deprived childhood bought for herself the little toys that her parents had denied her. With each toy, she felt satisfied, especially when she acknowledged her gifts were *to her inner child.*

We can call our souls home in a number of ways: traditional psychotherapy, workshops and seminars, reading, imagery (seeing ourselves in positive ways) and emotional honesty in our relationships. A healing relationship often helps the process.

When we feel stuck at a given point, a most effective way of inviting our soul to return home is by physically going to the place of origin and utilizing the power of place in a *ritual of healing.*

A young man returned to his home town and, as he walked the streets, he began to relive some of his history. He tells his story:

"I could see my Dad, even though he's dead now, striding next to me. It was the same way as our last walk together. He asked me, 'How far do you think it is to the next house? Think we could hit it with this stone? How fast would the stone have to travel to hit it in five minutes?'

"I said, 'No, Dad. That's not what I want to hear. I want to ask you this: How do I stay strong enough to trust when my trust is betrayed? Where do I put my rage when this happens? Do you really love me? Am I all you wanted me to be?'

"I realized that I was there to take my soul back. I went to the place where I had felt the closest to my father. I had taken with me a slide-rule my Dad had given me because he wanted me to be an engineer. (I am an artist.) I spoke to him of the things that I was most conflicted about. I buried the slide-rule in that place.

"I returned his slide-rule to him and decided not to live out his life and fulfill his dreams. I said a prayer for him and for me while I buried it. When I finished, I felt less empty and more complete than ever before. I felt more peaceful but not fully finished. Guess I'll have to return to my Dad whenever I feel the need, until all of my soul is back home."

There are also many healing practices we can incorporate into our daily life. Here are some I've learned:

1. Create a sacred space in a room or a corner of your home. Collect a few objects, such as statues, pictures and the like — things you may have purchased which symbolize something special to you. Or use objects such as feathers, stones, pieces of trees or leaves you may have picked up in nature. Then sit in your sacred space daily when you meditate.

2. Create a notebook of words, phrases, affirmations that resonate with your heart and soul. Add to it and remove the ones you're finished with.

3. Make a visual, concrete word or picture of your small successes. Physical: I learned to play golf today. Emotional: I got in touch with my sadness. Social: I learned to say no. Financial: I can manage my money better now than before.

4. Remember to thank God daily for: food, water, shelter, a sunrise, a lovely fall moon, the snow...

5. Give away something you don't use to someone you know. Or wrap it up in gift paper when you give it to a charitable organization and don't use this one as a tax deduction. Don't tell anyone you've done this.

6. Play music you love and dance to it when the mood strikes you.

7. Learn parenting/nurturing skills by watching children. Would you treat a little child in the ways you treat

yourself? Would you say to a little child the things you say to yourself?

8. When you care for your body, take time to enjoy the care you give yourself.

9. Learn Quiet-the-mind techniques such as meditation, yoga or martial arts (Tai Chi Chuan).

10. Go for walks in nature. Notice what you see, hear and smell.

11. For no reason, do any one of the following things that make you feel good:

Sit by the lake. Listen to music you love. Laugh. Sit in the sun without moving for five to ten minutes. Sing out loud. Scream out loud when you feel tense.

Get a new haircut. Hug a child. Keep conscious contact with your emotional and spiritual selves. Develop an ongoing relationship with God as you understand Him/Her. If you concentrate on feeling good, you can think of many more things to do for yourself.

Soul return rituals are very simple. They need to be done every day. There is no magical cure but these ways of self-care, soul-care provide concrete and real ways to do the work of recovery.

Through our work together in this book, we have met and shared an important part of life and recovery. Now we must part. I feel sad at the moment of our parting, though I know we will meet again. What can I give to you at this moment?

a tear?

a joke?

a tender sigh?

a bit of myself to carry away with you?

May you be kissed by the Light.

THE LIGHT

A dark night
  raining
    cold
      deep
        dangerous.
The darkness of fear covers my soul. I weep and bow my head
in silent supplication.
Look! The Light appears!
The Light shines through
the ice-covered trees, crystallized in time.
We are all magically transformed by the glowing Light
into diamonds of great beauty and value: Gold, Silver, Pink.
Shapes frozen in time and place.
Even the once-ugly mounds of dirt
Transformed ...
By the flowing Light.
My soul opens its eyes and sings its song ...
Transformed am I into Beauty and Color and Light.
Shimmering and shining for all to see.

—Dorothy

APPENDIX A

DEFINITIONS OF CODEPENDENCY

Codependency is a failure to complete two most important tasks of childhood: autonomy and intimacy.

It is about lack of problem solving skills.

It is a deep dependence on others.

It is a set of rigid rules we follow.

It is about needing validation from outside sources.

It is about denial of self for the sake of feeling connected to others.

It is trying to control by one's own will power.

It is a confusion of identities - identifying too much and too thoroughly with another.

It is about infant domination over the environment - King Baby.

It is about an addictive process in the society, between people and within a person

A codependent has let another person's behavior affect him and is obsessed with controlling that person's behavior.

It is other-centeredness.

It is a normal response to abnormal people.

Codependency shows up in boundary difficulties.

Codependency is living in the extremes. It is exaggerated behavior.

Codependency is the root addiction of all - a disempowerment that creates a final alienation from all that gives life meaning.

It is about faulty separation and attachment - a failure in individuation.

It is a process with a traceable path and a trajectory with a predictable outcome.

It is a societal failure to teach children the self- development and personal empowerment necessary to direct their lives in a meaningful manner.

Recovery from codependency is the willingness to abandon and be abandoned.

Recovery from codependency is creating a new consciousness.

APPENDIX B

FEELING-SYMPTOMS OF SOULLOSS

Feelings-Symptoms include:

A black hole that follows me everywhere and reappears consistently.

No matter how much I achieve, I feel empty.

No matter what I do, I feel haunted, restless, incomplete.

I don't feel like myself.

I don't know who I am.

I can't connect with others.

I over-attach to others.

I think I am bad, flawed, filled with shame and guilt.

I have low energy and feel listless, bored and dull.

I am scared, angry or numb most of the time.

I am dispirited and disheartened.

APPENDIX C

PATTERNS OF COMPLIANT CODEPENDENCY

My good feelings about who I am stem from being liked by you.

My good feelings about who I am stem from receiving approval from you.

Your struggle affects my serenity. My mental attention focuses on solving your problems.

My mental attention is focused on pleasing you.

My mental attention is focused on protecting you.

My mental attention is focused on manipulating you.

My self-esteem is bolstered by solving your problems

My self-esteem is bolstered by relieving your pain.

My own hobbies and interests are put aside. My time is spent sharing your interests and your hobbies.

Your clothing and personal appearance are top priority with me as I feel you are a reflection of me. My behavior is dictated by your desires.

I am not aware of how I feel. I am aware of how you feel.

I am not aware of what I want. I ask what you want.

The dreams I have for my future are linked to you.

My fear of rejection determines what I say or do.

My fear of abandonment determines what I say or do.

My fear of your anger determines what I say or do.

I use giving as a way of feeling safe in our relationship.

I use giving as a means of controlling you.

My social circle diminishes as I involve myself with you.

I put my values aside in order to connect with you.

I value your opinion and way of doing things more than my own.

The quality of my life is in relation to the quality of yours.

— From *Codependents Anonymous Self Help Groups*

APPENDIX D

PATTERNS OF CONTROLLING CODEPENDENCY

My mental attention is focused on pleasing myself and escaping into (chemicals, work, TV, etc.).

My mental attention is focused on controlling you. If I don't control you, I think I will lose you.

My mental attention is focused on manipulating you, to force you to do it my way...often with my temper, with logic or with money.

My self esteem is bolstered by solving your problems. If you don't ask for my opinion, I feel left out.

I want to spend *all* of my time with you and I want you to do the same. But I will tell you that I don't need you.

I am not aware of how you feel. I am not aware of how I feel.

I am not aware of what you want. I am not aware of what I want.

The dreams I have for my future are linked to you.

My fear of rejection determines what I say or do. I hide it under anger, bluster, pride, domination.

I use my anger as a way of controlling others and distancing you.

I use giving (often material things) as a way of feeling safe and controlling you. If I am in control, you will not leave me.

My social circle diminishes as I involve myself with my escape routes (chemical, TV, work, etc.)

I feel vulnerable when you come too close to me. But don't go away.

I value my own opinions and way of doing things more than yours.

I have few hobbies and interests other than my escape routes.

Your behavior is dictated by my desires, as I feel you are a reflection of me.

I assume I know what you want and what is good for you. I know what is best for you.

I assume others think and feel the same as I do and I can't understand nor accept differences.

I'm too proud to ask for your help. I'll never be dependent on you. I'll never tell you that I need you.

I had a hard time as a kid and I survived. A person has to be tough in a tough world. If you are tender, I take it as a sign of weakness.

If you talk about what's going on with you emotionally, it will be a reflection on me. Keep your mouth shut.

—*Dorothy May, Ph.D.*

APPENDIX E

POSITIVE AFFIRMATIONS

Just for today I will respect my own and others' boundaries.

Just for today I will be vulnerable with someone I trust.

Just for today I will take one compliment and hold it in my heart for more than a fleeting moment. I will take a deep breath and let it nurture me.

Just for today I will act in a way that I would admire in someone else.

I am a child of God.

I am a precious person.

I am a worthwhile person.

I am beautiful inside and outside.

I love myself unconditionally.

I can allow myself ample leisure time without feeling guilty.

I deserve to be loved by myself and others.

I am loved because I deserve love.

I deserve love, peace, prosperity and serenity.

I forgive myself for hurting myself and others.

I forgive myself for accepting sex when I wanted love.

I am willing to accept love.

I am not alone. I am one with God and the universe.

I am whole and good.

I am capable of changing.

The pain that I might feel by remembering can't be any worse than the pain I feel by knowing and not remembering.

—*Codependents Anonymous, 1988*

APPENDIX F

RESOURCES FOR MORE INFORMATION

ACOA Intergroup of Greater New York
P.O. Box 363 Murray Hill Station
New York, NY 10016-0363
(212) 582-0840

Adult Children of Alcoholics (AC0A)
2225 Sepulveda Blvd., #200
Torrance, CA 90505
(213) 534-1858

Al-Anon Family Service Group Headquarters
P.O. Box 862 Midtown Station
New York, NY 10018-0862
(212) 302-7240

Alcoholics Anonymous World Services, Inc.
768 Park Ave., South
New York, NY 10016
(212) 686-1100

Cocaine Anonymous
3740 Overland Ave. Suite G
Los Angeles, CA 90034
800-347-8998

Codependents Anonymous
P.O. Box 33577
Phoenix, AZ 85067-3577
(602) 277-7991

Debtors Anonymous General Service Board
P.O. Box 20322
New York, NY 10025-9992
(212) 969-0710

Drugs Anonymous
P.O. Box 473 Ansonia Station
New York, NY 10023
(212) 874-0700

Families Anonymous, Inc.
  P.O. Box 528
  Van Nuys, CA 91408
  (818) 989-7841

Gamblers Anonymous National Service Office
  P.O. Box 17173
  Los Angeles, CA 90017
  (213) 386-8789

Incest Survivors Anonymous Information Exchange
  P.O. Box 3399
  New Haven, CT 06515
  (203) 389-5166

Narcotics Anonymous World Services Office
  16155 Wyandotte St.
  Van Nuys, CA 91406
  (818) 780-3951

National Association of Adult Children of Dysfunctional Families
  Box 463
  Fond du Lac, WI 54935

National Association for Children of Alcoholics
  31582 Coast Highway, #201
  South Laguna, CA 92677
  (714) 499-3889

National Clearinghouse for Alcohol and Drug Information
  P.O. Box 2345
  Rockville, MD 20852

National Wellness Institute South Hall
  1319 Fremont St.
  Stevens Pt., WI 54481

Overeaters Anonymous
  4025 Spender St. #203
  Torrance, CA 90503
  (213) 542-8363

Sex Addicts Anonymous
  Box 3038
  Minneapolis, MN 55403
  (612) 339-0217

Sexaholics Anonymous
  P.O. Box 300
  Simi Valley, CA 93062
  (805) 339-0217

Sex and Love Addicts Anonymous
  The Augustine Fellowship
  P.O. Box 119 New Town Branch
  Boston, MA 02258
  (617) 332-1845

Smokers Anonymous
  2118 Greenwich St.
  San Francisco, CA 94123

Survivors of Incest Anonymous
  P.O. Box 21817
  Baltimore, MD 21222-6817
  (301) 282-3400

LOCAL RESOURCES:

AA Chicago: 312-346-1475

ACOA Chicago: 312-929-4581

FA Chicago: 312-777-4442

GA Chicago: 312-346-1588

OA Chicago: 312-202-4590

VOICES for Illinois Children: 312-456-0600

IF YOU WOULD LIKE TO CONTACT US:

Dorothy May, PhD
Whales' Tales Press
160 Wildwood
Lake Forest, IL 60045
1-800-428-9507

Institute for Recovery
420 Lake Cook Rd.
Suite 107
Deerfield, IL 60015
Dr. Kathleen Whalen FitzGerald
(708) 680-2336

REFERENCES

Biereg, Sandy. "Transforming the Co-dependent Woman." 1991. *Health Communications*, Deerfield Beach, FL.

Beatie, Melodie. *Codependent No More.* 1987. Hazelden, MN.

Becnel, B.C. *The Co-Dependent Parent.* 1991. Lowell House, Los Angeles, CA.

Black, C. "It Will Never Happen To Me!" 1981. MAC Publ. Denver, CO.

Blume, ES. "Secret Survivors." 1990. Wiley & Sons. NY

Bradshaw, "J. Bradshaw on: The Family." 1988. *Health Communications.*

Bradshaw, J. "Healing the Shame that Binds You." 1989. *Health Communications.*

Branden, N. *If You Could Hear What I Cannot Say.* 1983. Bantam, NY

Brende, J.O. *Post-Traumatic Stress Disorder and the War Veteran Patient.* 1985. Brunner/Mazel, NY

Beck, R. Metrick, S.B. *The Art of Ritual.* 1990. Celestial Arts. Berkeley, CA.

Bass, E. Davis, L. *The Courage to Heal.* 1993. HarperCollins, NY

Benson, H. *Beyond the Relaxation Response.* 1985. Berkley Books, NY

Briggs, D.C. *Celebrate Yourself.* 1977. Doubleday, NY

Bloomfield, H. Felder, L. *Making Peace with Your Parents.* 1983. Random House, NY

Bryan, M. Cameron, J. *Money Drunk.* 1992. Ballantine, NY

Capacchione, L. *Recovery of Your Inner Child.* 1991. Simon & Schuster Fireside, NY

Castine, J. "Recovery From Rescuing" 1989. *Health Communications.*

Cermak, T. L. "A Primer on Adult Children of Alcoholics." 1985. *Health Communications.*

Chandler, M. "Gentle Reminders for Co-dependents." 1989. *Health Communications.*

"Codependency. Anthology". 1985, 1990. *Health Communications.*

Cork, M. "The Forgotten Children." 1969. *Addiction Research Foundation,* Toronto, Canada.

Courtois, C.A. *Healing the Incest Wound.* 1988. WW Norton, NY

Covington, S. Beckett, L. *Leaving the Enchanted Forest.* 1988. Harper & Row, San Francisco, CA

Cruse, J.R. "Painful Affairs". 1989. *Health Communications.*

Dean, Amy. *Making Changes: How Adult Children Can Have Healthier, Happier Relationships.* 1989. Hazelden, MN.

Earle, et al. *Lonely All the Time.* 1989. Simon & Schuster, NY.

Evans, G. *The Wall.* 1977. Word Books, Waco, TX.

Elkin, M. *Families Under the Influence.* 1984. WW Norton, NY.

Ellsworth, BA. "Living in Love with Yourself". 1988. BreakThrough Publ. Salt Lake City, UT

Ferrucci, P. *What We May Be.* 1980. JP Tarcher, Los Angeles, CA.

Fishel, R. "Healing Energy." 1991. *Health Communications.*

FitzGerald, Kathleen W. Ph.D. *Alcoholism: The Genetic Inheritance.* 1993. Whales' Tales Press, Lake Forest, IL.

Forward, S. Torres J. *Men Who Hate Women and the Women Who Love Them.* 1986. Bantam, NY.

Friel, J, Friel, L. "Adult Children: The Secrets of Dysfunctional Families." 1988. *Health Communications.*

Gawain, S. *Creative Visualization.* 1982. Bantam Books, NY.

Groom, N. *From Bondage to Bonding: A Working Guide to Recovery from Codependency.* 1992. Nav. Press.

Gendlen, E. *Focusing.* 1981. Bantam Books, NY.

Greenleaf, J. "Co-alcoholic, Para-alcoholic: Who's Who." 1981. *MAC Publ.* Denver, CO.

Gravitz, H. Bowden, J. *Guide to Recovery.* 1985. Simon & Schuster.

Halliday, L. "The Silent Scream." 1981. *Sexual Abuse Victims Anonymous,* Canada.

Halpern, H. *How to Break Your Addiction to a Person.* 1982. Bantam, NY.

Harman, W. Hormann, J. "Creative Work." 1990. Knowledge Systems, Indianapolis, IN.

Harris, B. Spiritual "Awakening: Healing into Unconditional Love." 1992. *Health Communications.*

Hayes, J. *Smart Love.* 1989. Tarcher, Los Angeles, CA

Hendrix, H. *Getting the Love You Want.* 1988. Harper & Row, NY

Hoffman, B. *No One Is to Blame.* 1979. Science & Behavior Books, Palo Alto, CA.

Houston, J. *The Search for the Beloved.* 1987. Tarcher, Los Angeles, CA.

Kellogg, T. "Broken Toys, Broken Dreams." 1990. *Recovery Res. Grp.*

Kasl, C. *Many Roads, One Journey.* 1992. Harper & Row, NY.

Kaye, Y. Credit, "Cash and Co-dependency." 1991. *Health Communications.*

Kritsberg, W. "The Adult Children of Alcoholics Syndrome." 1985. *Health Communications.*

Kritsberg, W. "Healing Together". 1990. *Health Communications.*

Kunzman, K.A. *The Healing Way.* 1990. Hazelden, MN.

Lamb, M. *Sibling Relationships.* 1982. Lawrence Erlbaum, Hillsdale, NJ.

Latimer, J. *Living Binge-Free.* 1990. Living Quest, Bounder.

LeBlanc, D. "You Can't Quit Until You Know What's Eating You". 1990. *Health Communications.*

Lee, J. "The Flying Boy, Healing the Wounded Man". 1990. *Health Communications.*

Leichtman, R. Japiske, C. *Active Meditation. The Western Tradition.* 1982. Ariel Press, Columbus, OH.

Love, P. with Robinson, J. *The Emotional Incest Syndrome.* 1990. Bantam, NY

Lerner, H. *The Dance of Anger.* 1985. Harper & Row, NY.

Lerner H. *The Dance of Intimacy.* 1989. Harper & Row, NY.

Missildine, W.H. *Your Inner Child of the Past.* 1991. Simon & Schuster, NY

Marlin, E. Hope: *New choices and recovery strategies for ACOAs.* 1987. Harper & Row, NY.

Maltz, Wendy. *Sexual Healing Journey.* 1991. Harper.

Meiselman, K. *Incest.* 1978. Jossey-Bass, San Francisco CA.

Mellody, P. Miller, A. & Miller, J. *Facing Codependency.* 1989. Harper.

Metzner, R. *Opening to Inner Light.* 1986. Tarcher, Los Angeles, CA.

Middelton-Moz, J. Dwinell, L. "After the Tears." 1986. *Health Communications.*

Miller, A. *The Drama of the Gifted Child.* 1981. Basic Books/Harper Colophon, NY.

Miller, A. *The Enabler.* 1988. Hunter House, Claremont, CA/Ballantine, NY.

Mumey, J. *Loving and Alcoholic.* 1988. Bantam, NY.

Namka, L. "The Doormat Syndrome." 1989. *Health Communications.*

Norwood, R. *Women who Love Too Much.* 1985. Tarcher, Los Angeles, CA.

Pearce, J. *Magical Child*. 1980. Bantam, NY.

Page, Penny. *Children of Alcoholics: A Sourcebook*. 1991. Garland.

Paladin, L. *Ceremonies for Change*. 1991. Stillpoint Publ., Walpole, NH.

Peabody, S. *Addiction to Love*. 1988. Ten Speed Press, Berkeley, CA.

Picard, F. *Family Intervention Ending the Cycle of Addiction and Codependency*. 1989. Beyond Words Publ. Inc., Hillsboro, OR.

Ram Dass, Gorman P. *How Can I Help?* 1985. AA Knopf, NY.

Ray, V. *Striking a Balance*. 1989. Hazelden, MN.

Ray, V. *Communicating with Love*. 1989. Hazelden, MN.

Reedy, B. McElfresh, O. *Detachment*. 1987. Parkside, Park Ridge, IL

Robinson, B. "Work Addiction." 1989. *Health Communications*.

Stoop, D. Masteller, J. *Forgiving our Parents, Forgiving Ourselves*. 1991. Vine Books.

Sanders, C. *Grief-The Mourning After*. 1989. John Wiley &Sons, NY.

Sanford, L. *The Silent Children*. 1980. Anchor Press/Doubleday, NY.

Sanford, L. *Strong at the Broken Places*. 1990. Prentice Hall, NY.

Satir, V. *The New Peoplemaking*. 1988. Science & Beh. Books.

Scarf, M. *Unfinished Business*. 1980. Random House, NY.

Schaef, A. *When Society Becomes an Addict*. 1987. Harper & Row, NY.

Schaeffer, B. *Is it Love or Is it Addiction?* 1987. Hazelden, MN.

Simons, G. *Keeping Your Personal Journal*. 1978. Paulist Press, NJ.

Simos, B. "A Time to Grieve." 1979. Fam. Svcs. Assoc. of America.

Sloat, D. *Growing up Holy and Wholly*. 1990. Wolgemuth & Hyatt, Brentwood, TN.

Small, J. *Awakening in Time*. 1991. Bantam, NY.

Small, J. *Becoming Naturally Therapeutic*. 1989. Bantam, NY.

Smith, A. "Grandchildren of Alcoholics." 1988. *Health Communications*.

Smith, A. "Overcoming Perfectionism. 1990. *Health Communications*.

Snow, C. Willard, D. *I'm Dying to Take Care of You*. 1989. Professional Counselor Books, Redmond, WA.

Stuart, M. "In Sickness and In Health Communications." 1988. *Health Communications*.

Subby, R. "Lost in the Shuffle". 1987. *Health Communications*.

Wolter, D. *Forgiving our Parents, for Adult Children from Dysfunctional Families*. 1989. Comp Care.

Wholey, D. *Becoming Your Own Parent*. 1990. Bantam, NY.

Woititz, J. "Adult Children of Alcoholics, Expanded". 1990. *Health Communications.*

Washton, A. Boundy, D. *Willpower's Not Enough.* 1989. Harper & Row, NY.

Wegscheider, S. "Another Chance: Hope and Health for the Alcoholic Family." 1981. Science & Behavior.

Wegscheider, S. "Choicemaking". 1985. *Health Communications.*

Wegscheider-Cruse. "Understanding Codependency." 1990. *Health Communications.*

Weil, A. *Natural Health, Natural Medicine.* 1990. Houghton Mifflin, NY.

Weiss, J. Weiss, L. "Recovery from Codependency". 1988. *Health Communications.*

Whitfield, C. "A Gift to Myself". 1990. *Health Communications.*

Whitfield, C. "Codependence: Healing the Human Condition". 1991. *Health Communications.*

Wills-Brandon, C. "Learning to Say No". 1990. *Health Communications.*

Wills-Brandon, C. "Where Do I Draw the Line?" 1991. *Health Communications.*

Windle, M. "Children of Alcoholics: A comprehensive bibliography". 1989. NY State Div. of Alcoholism & Alcohol Abuse, Buffalo, NY.

Wotitz, J. "Struggle for Intimacy." 1985. *Health Communications.*

INDEX